A LITTLE SEX
A LOT OF DOPE
AND AN AIRCRAFT CARRIER

an unauthorized naval history by Cap'n Drift

A LITTLE SEX
A LOT OF DOPE
AND AN AIRCRAFT CARRIER

It is not the intention of this book to condone or promote
irresponsible drug use. The scenes in this book are merely a
recounting of events that happened in that place at that time.

Nothing more.   - Cap'n Drift

Litsam
for the books!

For the men and women currently working the flight decks of our carriers: keep your head up and your hands out of your pockets.

See ya when you get home.

And finally, to the fellas who were there: write your own damned book.

Copyright © Nov. 30, 2010 Cap'n Drift
Published Dec. 2011, Litsam Inc.
All rights reserved.

ISBN-13: 978-1-935878-04-9
ISBN-10: 1-935878-04-2
E-book ISBN: 978-1-935878-05-6

This is a creative work. Names and stories, fictional and factual, are rendered from the author's imagination. Any semblance to persons living or dead, or events past present or future, is entirely coincidental. Truth is an unfolding story.

Published by Litsam, Inc.
Shoreline, WA U.S.A.
http://www.litsam.com

PROLOGUE

I had intended to start this out from August of 1976. That was when I joined the Navy. Well, I suppose it wasn't really the Navy. It was the Navy Reserves. The agreement was I'd do three years of active duty and then three years as a weekend warrior. Things turned out a touch different than that, but in the end it turned out good for both me and the Navy. I sorta, kinda, feel like I need to explain the events that led to my enlistment. We'll need to go back eight or nine years.

I'll try to make it brief.

Before the Boat

I spent half of my young life in foster homes. No, no, I'm not crying in my beer over here. I'm merely giving you some background. Probably half of my early childhood was spent with my aunt and uncle or dumped off somewhere else. I once spent two days with a Mexican family that didn't speak English. The remaining time, it was just me and the Ol' Man. Oh, well, there was that period with the Evil Stepmom, too…

The Ol' Man was an engineer for the Southern Pacific Railroad. He was also a drunk.

It was when he and I were living at the Linden Hotel in downtown El Paso that he got arrested for whoring. I had thought he saved that for when he took me for a haircut over in Juarez; obviously not. They took him to jail and me to a foster home. I was about nine years old at the time.

He got out of jail, and I scooted away from the temporary home. I jumped into his T-bird and we headed to Yuma, Arizona, where we set up at the Del Sol Hotel in downtown and he kept driving trains for the Southern Pacific. The S.P. frowns on their engineers being drunk while operating their locomotives. The Ol' Man got busted.

The Ol' Man got canned.

I think it was when he held my puppy out of the third story window of our hotel room that I decided to run away. I'd found his partial bottle of whiskey and hid it. Since he was already drunk, I thought maybe he'd think he had finished it and pass out. It had worked before.

He told me if I didn't tell him where I'd put the booze, he was going to drop the dog. I handed him his bottle.

The railroad bulls caught me in the yard, hopping an eastbound freight. With me I had a half-loaf of bread, another bread sack with maybe a pound of pecans in it, and two root beers. I don't recall what I had for money. I'll bet something shiny it wasn't more than ten bucks though.

I was headed for El Paso. Downtown El Paso, actually. You see, I knew the layout. I had been friends with some of the Mexican shoeshine boys when we lived at the Linden. I figured I'd put together a box and hustle and hide. The bulls hauled me off to juvenile hall and called the Ol' Man.

He told 'em to keep me. I spent the next eight years in three different foster homes.

The first was the Quills, Gladys and Sylvanious. They called Sylvanious "Shorty."

Shorty and Gladys were older retired folks. Gladys kept house and Shorty puttered around. They were raising Chinchillas for pelts, but that never really worked out. They didn't like killing them.

When I arrived, there was another cat already living there. His name was Ronny.

Ronny was one of those kids they poured the Ritalin to. There was that time when I had to beat him up to keep him from jumping from the radio tower with a flare parachute. I'm not sure where the 'chute came from. It wasn't more than fifteen feet in diameter, and a bit rough for wear. Ronny was quite sure he could BASE jump from the 125-foot tower down the street with it.

Once I knocked him off his feet with a rock I had thrown through the corner of a chain link fence. Yeah, like through the fence, twice, clean. That wasn't about any lifesaving. I was just being mean. We had a "brother" type relationship. They do that, right? Brothers. Be mean.

We called Gladys and Shorty "Grandma" and "Grandpa."

They took in all types of kids. Sometimes kids would show up without any shoes. Sometimes they'd arrive in their pajamas. There was the deaf kid who would come and hang out whenever it was school holiday. I haven't the foggiest what that was about.

I've since forgotten the technique, but at one time I was pretty quick with the hand alphabet. We'd get in trouble for using it in front of grandpa and grandma. They didn't like not knowing what we were "saying." Ronny never really picked it up. Oh, just enough to tell when we were making fun of him, but not enough to truly understand or "talk." He would make ridiculous hand flopping gestures and I'd ask what the hell it was supposed to mean. Deaf dude would be standing there looking at me shaking his head in confusion. I'd ask Ronny what the hell he was doing.

"Nobody knows but me."

Ronny was fucked up in the head and feeling left out.

After he left I felt bad about the times I had been mean to him.

It's funny—the deaf kid was, uh, deaf, but when the dog would scratch at the door he would get up and let him in. I gave thought to whether he was bullshitting. You know? If he really *could* hear. I sit here, forty years later and near deaf. He wasn't bullshitting. It's all about vibrations, man.

Some would be there for a day or two before one of their parents would bail out, or whatever, and off they'd go. I seem to recall, on one occasion, a kid arriving in the morning and leaving that evening. Ronny and I were the regulars. Then, after a couple of years, Ronny split. His mom finally got her act together, or some shit. Ronny was gone.

It bummed me, man.

The Quills quit taking in the transients. The Quills quit taking me in. When they told me, I cried for two days. I mean two days solid. I had flourished there. It was my home. It was a regular fucking home.

I was an honor student. I was on the student council. I was the goddamned sixth grade class president!

I was still crying when the caseworker came to take me to my new residence. I was about thirteen years old. That was my age when something in my mind broke, I'm pretty sure. Yeah, it was then... pretty sure. Limits. Over the edge.

Fucking *twang*, man.

I moved in with the Jones family: Al, Alice and their son Matt. Matt was a couple of years older than me.

Me and Alice got off to a bad start right off of the bat. I had asked her what I was supposed to call her and she said, "Mom."

I replied that though I had never known my mother I was pretty damned sure she wasn't her and I would call her Alice.

The fan had been turned on. The aroma of feces was prevalent in the air.

About three years later, one stolen and wrecked car, one charge of prescribing medicines without a license (didn't stick) and a couple charges of incorrigibility, there was a knock at the kitchen door while I was making a peanut butter sandwich. It was a cop.

"Are you James Kennedy?"

Don't you just hate that? Fuck, I hate that!

The Joneses had kicked me out.

When I arrived at juvenile hall, the new one this time, my case-worker was waiting for me. When I asked her what I was there for she said, "Forever."

Basically, the gig was that without a home I was headed for the big house. That would be Fort Grant, the Juvenile Joint. I would live there until my eighteenth birthday. Things were looking rather bleak.

But I had friends. Yeah, as screwed up as I was, I still had friends. It was those friends who saved my ass.

Pat and Whitey and Booty went to Pat's uncle Hank and told him of my plight. They pretty much told him the truth. You know, "He's a little rough around the edges, but basically a good kid. He just needs a chance."

To this day I don't know why, but Pop (I came to call him Pop) plucked me from the hall as one might salvage a condemned puppy from the pound.

I can't begin to tell you what I learned from this, man. I can't begin to tell you what effect he had on my life. That said, after reading on a bit further you might be asking yourself exactly what it was I did learn. It took a few years to sink in, okay?

I was at his side when he died a couple of years back. I wish I could have given him something more.

As I've implied, I went home with Hank and his wife Betty. I was about sixteen and a half.

When I turned eighteen, they didn't give me the boot. Instead, they bought a small camp trailer for me. You could go from one end to the other in three little steps or two big ones. It had a sink and a stove but no shower or shitter. Over time I repaid them for the price of the trailer, and that was about it.

There were rules though, one being no women. She was loud. I got busted.

The next day while we were out in the shop Pop told me that Betty had said the next time it happened one of us (he or me) would have to go.

Did I mention Pop and Betty's bedroom window was about six feet from mine? Did I say already that the gal was loud? I guess it made an impression on Betty.

I moved in with Buck. We were working together "rogueing in the wheat" for the Northrup King Seed Company. Prior to harvest, people walk down the rows of plants and yank out anything that isn't the crop. It's like weeding, I reckon. That's how they can claim the seed is 99.99 percent pure.

The wheat plants would shred a pair of jeans in about two weeks. Buck was recently married and his missus was with child.

My stay there didn't last long. The season ended, too, and I was without a job.

Terry and I got an apartment. Terry is Buck's brother. We go back before the whole "rot in juvy" thing.

Actually, it was me, Terry and his ol' lady Sis who got an apartment. That didn't work out entirely great, either.

Money: You need money to pay the bills and buy food. Hey, being young is a learning curve, right? I recall once running out of food after eating nothing but potatoes for four days. No money. No food. Desperation.

It seemed to me the solution was a no-brainer. I think it was about one o'clock in the morning when I changed my clothes to dark colors. I grabbed my backpack and several paper shopping bags out of the kitchen. I could find only one glove, so I slipped a sock over the other hand. Terry asked me what the hell I was doing.

"Going grocery shopping," I responded.

There was a small market over on the corner. I kicked out the bottom of the glass door. At first, I tried cutting the glass with the cutter I had taken with me. After about the third attempt with no success, frustration got the best of me.

I stepped back and gave it the boot. Then I ran and hid in the bushes and waited. Nothing: no alarms, no cops, nothing.

So I went shopping. I didn't bother to check the cash register. Hell, I don't think I even took any cigarettes. Food, man. I wanted food.

Because the damned upper glass portion of the door slid down while I was inside, I had to kick my way back out. I then ferried my bags to a safe location. Terry helped me get them home from there.

This being out on your own crap wasn't turning out like I thought it would.

I copped a job at a gas station across the Colorado River in Winterhaven, where I met the two cats I would lead on a crime spree in San Diego.

They were hitchhikers. There was some story about the one cat losing his panel truck during a big holiday weekend at a local water reservoir, Senator's Wash, which was a recreational site known for a party *place*. They had come back to do whatever it was they had to do to get the truck. Impound fees, towing, fines, I don't know. That was a long time ago.

I invited them to spend the night at our place. Terry and Sis were not amused. The next day I lost my job. I don't think I worked at the station for more than a week.

The owner dude was on me about holes in the knees of my jeans. I simply responded that when I got a paycheck, I'd be able to buy a new pair. It wasn't like I was being a smartass or anything. No money, no jeans—simple as that.

That night, I fucked up the till somehow. I didn't steal anything. I screwed up a propane sale. I wasn't supposed to ring it up or something... Like I said, it was a long time ago, I don't recall the details.

Owner dude canned me. Terry and Sis were... well, you get it.

Hitchhiker cats didn't get the truck. There was a problem. Again, I don't remember what the deal was. They felt the heat from the other residents of the home and decided it would be best if they split. Having lost my job I figured I'd take a short vacation and head off to San Diego with them. We hit the highway onramp with our thumbs out.

I suppose I oughtta give the hitchhiker cats names. It'd be tough to continue the story otherwise. What names do you like? Hmm, let's see… How about Mike and Jeff? Too late; I've decided.

We'll call Mike the more aggressive of the two, the extrovert. Jeff was the mellower of the pair.

We landed at Mike's place. Actually, it was his older brother's place. The brother was out of town on a job or some shit. It was the next afternoon that I learned the house was near a high school. At lunch time, a few little bebop gals came over to get stoned. It didn't happen because we didn't have any weed. They didn't get high. We didn't get laid.

Bummer.

There wasn't any fuckin' food in Mike's brother's house. We were all broke, too. That going hungry shit was getting old. We headed downtown to the servicemen's club to pull a scam. It was the ol' "peddling weed that we didn't have" ruse. We could only do it once, and then we'd have to disappear.

It was Mike's idea.

There was an interior door to the building that locked in the wrong direction. That is, it could be opened from the alley side but not from the inside. We opened it and blocked it, and then started looking for our fish.

Mike took dude's money and I stayed with dude. You know, that way the mark feels like everything is on the up and up. After I was satisfied that Mike had enough time to get to our prearranged meeting place, I pushed the mark down the steps and ran like hell for the door. I kicked the wedge out of it and slammed it behind me on my way through. I met Mike and Jeff at McDonalds.

We pigged out.

That night, we decided to go to La Jolla. The events of the evening are a bit jumbled in my memory. This I do know: that night I stole a panel truck, a Baja bug and a motorcycle, and broke into the office of a miniature golf place. It started when we ran out of bus fare. There was nothing left from the day's earlier take. We were afoot. I spied an old panel truck sitting on a dark street.

Having a mechanical background, along with previous car theft experience, I knew hot wiring it would be a piece of cake. Screw that walking shit.

We got to the beach and the clutch went out of it.

We were hoofing it again. This time around, I took the bug. We abandoned it somewhere, I think. That part is really foggy. We were trudging along once again when we came upon the miniature golf outfit. I pried the lock off with some tool I had found lying around.

We filled bags with candy. No, man, seriously: it was a candy heist.

When we came upon the dirt bike, we dumped the sweets. It was sitting in sort of an alleyway behind some apartments. It was like a swap; Butter Fingers for sticky fingers. I pushed it down the block, fired it up, and all three of us rode it back to Mike's. Mike knew the back ways through canyons and storm water canals.

I decided it was time for me to get out of San Diego. Just by happenstance, Mike had a buddy with a pickup truck that was headed Yuma way. We loaded up the bike and off we went. I'm not sure why they accompanied me. Maybe it was something about still attempting to recover Mike's rig?

It was my first night back that the shit really hit the fan.

It was around midnight when Mike kept pestering me about riding that damned bike. I tried to explain that we would take it out to the desert the following day and ride the piss out of it. He wasn't having any of it. He wanted to ride it then and there. Finally I acquiesced telling him to push the fucking thing down the street before he started it. A 250 two stroke bike running wild in the neighborhood at midnight didn't seem like a very good idea to me but I was tired of arguing. At one point it almost turned physical.

"Fuck it, man," I said. "Go ride the damned thing, you fucking idiot."

Mike left and I got in the shower to cool down. Terry had already gone to bed in disgust with the whole situation. I think Sis had split back to her parent's home while I was in California.

Smart girl.

I suppose this is where I should introduce my girlfriend at the time, Collette. I suppose I have to. She's critical to the next part of the story.

I had bought her about a year earlier from her brother, Whitey.

I was over at his place while he worked on his truck and he kept bumming smokes from me. I had a carton in my Volvo so I went to give him a pack.

He wouldn't have it. He said he'd buy 'em from me.

About that time Collette walked out of the door and Whitey said, "Hell, I'll trade you my sister for 'em."

I asked her if she was alright with the trade. When she said she was good, it was a done deal. I'd bought me a girlfriend for the price of a pack of smokes.

I didn't even really know her. Oh sure, she was Whitey's sister and all, but it wasn't like I had ever sat and had a conversation with her. I knew that she generally kept to herself. I knew the other kids in the crowd thought she was a bit, uh, different. I knew she had given her stepmom a fat lip and black eye in a fist fight. I also knew she was a hot little motherfucker. Hell, at the time I thought it was just a joke. She didn't think it was a joke.

Collette took my cherry.

I'm confessing myself to be a liar with that revelation. See, for years I've been telling a story about a young whore down in Mexico being my first. It makes for a nice story, but it ain't true.

It was Collette, not the whore, who took my virginity.

I had to introduce her at this juncture because she was in the apartment that night. She spent many nights there. She was fifteen at that time. We had gone from screwing at the drive-in to semi-shacked up.

I had just stepped out of the shower when Collette walked into the bathroom.

"The cops are here and they want to talk to you about that bike."

That certainly sucked.

"I'll be right out. Don't let 'em in the apartment," I told her.

She tells me, "Too late. They're standing in the living room."

That was massive suckage. Waaaay fucking massive. Chaunce, that would be Terry—I call him Chaunce, he me Holmes, which has to do with an acid trip, the details of which aren't relevant to this particular story.

Anyway, Chaunce was dealing weed. He had been bagging it up in the living room before he went to bed. On the coffee table were scales, baggies, pot…

I thought about going out of the bathroom window, then decided screw it, I'd face whatever lay before me. It wasn't just because all I had to wear was a towel. After all, it was summer.

I thought maybe I could talk my way out of it. I figured that was better than running. It got more interesting than that. Though I suppose I did.

Talk my way out of it, that is.

When they stopped Mike, the cops had run the bike. Now this is a trip. It did come up stolen, but not from when I stole the damned thing. It had been stolen previously a year to the day.

I swiped a hot bike!

They cuffed me and took me to the jail house, and then things took a bit of a twist. While I was sitting in an interrogation room with the two coppers, the one told me they had got me on the following charges: grand theft, possession, possession for sale, contributing to the delinquency of a minor and interstate transportation of stolen property.

That interstate thing was a federal beef, by the way.

Fuck-oh-dear… I'm so goddamned hosed.

That's when copper dude One made the proposition.

He was transferring to narcotics, you see. He could use a snitch.

Now, I hadn't been booked yet. No photo. No prints. Nothing but a sit down with "wannabe-a-narco" dude. I couldn't believe my ears. I was flabbergasted.

I asked, "Now let me make sure I've got this straight. You're telling me if I say I'll snitch for you I can walk out of here right now? I mean, get up and walk out."

He replied that Mike was a bad guy. He had a history. A violent, mental, career criminal kind of history. They had caught him with stolen property. They were happy. With me they would deal.

It was on the table.

I said, "Fuck yeah!," and walked out.

Obviously, Jeff split back to San Diego.

It was about a week later I was screwing around with my Volvo…

My Volvo was a 1960 544. Pop had bought a body, sans engine, and various other bits and given it to me. His nephew, Robbie, had a Volvo engine he was taking out of a dune buggy. I gave him two hundred bucks for it. The fenders were cut back; I had "meats" and wheels on it. The interior was old, worn, diamond tuck and roll. I had a Hurst shifter handle. It made it go faster, I swear. If I opened the deck lid and put three (heavy) people in the trunk, their legs dangling out, I could pop a six inch wheelie.

I'm getting lost here in the reminiscing. The car was a piece of shit. I don't know why I've such fond memories.

So I'm out shining my SU carburetors or some crap, and a black and white pulls up. Yep, it's my new copper buddy. He wants the scoop. Fuck, shit, piss, motherfucker. This fucking idiot really thinks this is going to happen. I tell him there's some cats that are about to move a couple of hundred pounds of weed up out of San Luis. I'd have the details in a couple of days and give him a call.

I also suggested he didn't stop by his snitch's place in a marked cruiser.

When the copper split, I walked into the apartment and told Chaunce I had to get out of Dodge. Again, as will repeat itself here time and time again, I don't recall the circumstances, but he said he was ready for a new venue himself.

We packed that night, jumped into his '56 (I think it was a '56) Chevy Bel Air and split for Merced, California. It gets kind of twisted and detail-ey so I'll spare you the half of a page it would take to explain the wheres and why-fors. The short version is Chaunce had an aunt up there. His sister was there as well. We hung out for a bit and then dropped down to Garden Grove with his sis and her very young daughter. Maw, Chaunce's mom, was living in Garden Grove.

We descended upon her like locusts.

After a few days, Chaunce's sister and her daughter took a bus out. Chaunce had been running around looking for work. I was stuck. I had no transportation in a strange town. I had no money. There was no fucking way I was going to find a job. I was sucking off of Maw's limited tit. Oh, she would have never thrown me out. I know that. I couldn't in good conscience continue as things were. It was a dead end.

I needed a plan.

Let's see… I had been on my own for less than a year. In that time, I had committed multiple crimes, gone hungry quite a bit, and was currently on the run from the law while mooching off of my buddy's mom.

It was quite obvious that a new strategy was called for.

I needed someone to feed me while I got my shit together. That was the main thing. That hungry shit really sucks. I don't care for hungry a'tall. I wasn't doing so well on my own. I needed some sort of a transitional period. I needed…

I decided to join the Navy. It was August of 1976. Yeah, we're there.

Almost.

WHERE DO I SIGN?

Chaunce gave me twenty cents. Maybe it was a dime. Yeah, I don't recall.

The deal was, we were under the impression that as long as you had money for a phone call you couldn't be picked up as a vagrant. I dunno. He gave me the dime(s) and dropped me off at the onramp. I was headed back to Yuma. I couldn't be there long. The copper, don't ya know.

I arrived in Yuma with one hell of a sunburn, five bucks, a full belly and two joints. The last cat who picked me up was a Navy vet and when I told him things had gone to shit and I was on my way to enlist, he took pity on me. He fed me, gave me the five bones and a chunk of his stash.

I got to Yuma to discover there wasn't a Navy recruiter in town anymore.

Fuck.

The closest office was in El Centro, California.

I was holed up at Collette's house. Okay, her dad's house.

For some *reason* Jerry Senior (Whitey being Junior) liked me. I know it doesn't make a lick of sense, but I believe he thought I was a good influence on his daughter.

I encouraged her to go to school. I helped her with homework. I discouraged her from fighting with her stepmom. It wasn't uncommon for Senior to ask me to talk to Collette about this and that. *I* could reach her. *I* could reason with her. As far as her parents went—she couldn't see reason.

Hell, that morning he caught me in her bed (I had sneaked in the window and fallen asleep beside her), Senior told me I had better not be there when the stepmom got up, and that he had breakfast going. When I told him I was going to enlist in the service, Jerry was more than happy to help me out.

The first stop was juvenile hall. The court and administration offices were in the same building. I was standing at the counter explaining to the help that I had heard a person could have their juvenile record expunged when the judge walked by; the same before whom I had stood on several occasions.

She caught part of the conversation and said, "Follow me."

I took the chair across from her desk and explained the Navy enlistment thing.

"You need to petition the court," she said. "Write a letter."

I was thinking, *crap-fuck-around, fuck-around,* when she tossed a writing tablet and a pen across her desk.

"Here, I'll tell you what to write." I wrote what she said.

"Sign and date it." I did.

She signed and dated as well, and then got up.

"Stay right there. I'll be back shortly."

She walked back in and tossed a one inch thick manila folder at me.

"You're expunged. Good luck."

I was shitting bricks the whole time I was there. I mean, it wasn't like I was at the county courthouse or the city cop station, but if "wanna-be-a-narco" dude happened to wander by, it would have been most inopportune.

Senior loaned me his Land Cruiser to go to El Centro. I walked in the door and told the recruiter to sign me up. 'Course it ain't that easy. There's the testing and talking and stuff. I did well on the testing.

I flunked the talking.

Once I admitted to smoking marijuana in the past, my ambitions of being an air traffic controller were dashed. My previous cannabis use constituted a "drug abuse history." Druggies couldn't be controllers. I settled for an aviation guarantee.

Then the son of a bitch told me I couldn't get in without a high school diploma or a GED. I had quit/been fired three quarters of the way through my senior year. They expelled me because my two-period auto shop class was the only one I had been attending. Working afternoons at the wrecking yard, I hadn't had time for that other "scholarly" crap.

He said the good news was he could set me up to take the GED test the following day. Yeah, great fucking news—at a facility in downtown San Diego.

Son of a bitch. Piss, fuck, motherfucker!

Fuck-around, fuck-around. I haven't a choice. I'm stuck. Will it be tomorrow, next week, when my stomach is empty again? I've got to do this. I've got to make it happen. I'll starve or go to prison if I don't make this happen.

I damn well knew it.

As luck would have it there was another cat at the recruiters that had set up to take the test. He lived in El Centro. I agreed to pick him up the following day on my way through. I hadn't any doubts that Senior would loan me his rig to go get it done. He kicked me the gas money, too. Though, as it turned out, we would be a little short.

The first bitch upon arriving was learning that you couldn't take all five tests in one day. They had to be split between a couple.

Them's the rules.

We spent the night in the Toyota, pointed the wrong way on a one way street. I had no idea until the next morning. As I was starting the rig, a friendly police officer pointed it out. He didn't cite me.

I flipped a bitch and headed for GED testing, Day Two.

The second bitch? It was quite obvious we hadn't the fuel or money to make it home. The Land Cruiser had guzzled a shitload more gas than I had anticipated.

Son of a bitch.

In my downtown travels, I'd spied a blood bank. It wasn't far from the GED testing place—or the Servicemen's Club for that matter.

I opted for the plasma bank.

I knew it would take a donation from both me and my companion to have enough dough to make it back. When I presented our predicament and my proposed solution to my fellow traveler, he freaked. He was one of those folks with the needle phobia thing. Wouldn't ya fuckin' know it?

After a bit of strong persuasion, he finally acquiesced. I put our blood money in the tank while hoping for a tailwind on the way home, and that the dude would quit whining. The way he was carrying on, you'd'a thought he'd lost a *lot* more than a pint of blood.

Now that I think back on it, I'm lucky I had the little pussy with me.

So now I had my GED and it was one more stop back at the recruiter's, where I picked up a bus ticket from Yuma to Los Angeles. Yeah, Senior helped me out with gas, a lot.

For the Yuma area, the intake center was (is?) in L.A. We were put up overnight in some fleabag hotel. Someone had a bottle and we got fuckered up.

I'm pretty sure it was Bob Davidson that produced the bottle of vodka. Bob Davidson? I know I've skipped over the how of it, cuz' I can't remember, but I joined up with Bob Davidson. We had gone to high school together. I must have run into him at the recruiter's office.

Must have...

Bob and I never really hung out together in school, but I'm thinking we figured a familiar face in boot camp would be advantageous.

I joined on the buddy system with Bob. Something they don't tell you about that is, if your buddy turns out to be a fuck-up and gets sent back in training, you go with him. After all, he's your buddy, right?

No, neither one of us turned out to be a fuck-up. Well, not individually. Our whole training company would turn out to be fuck-ups.

The next day was all about standing in line for this, that, and the other thing.

We were in a line for a blood draw and they couldn't find a vein on Bob. He asked several times that they hand him the rig, but they declined. Finally, he "guided" them to the right spot and depth—Bob having had quite a bit of experience with sinking a needle into that particular vein.

We stood with our pants at our ankles while a doc ran down the line instructing us, "Turn your head and cough." Maybe there was more than one bottle the night before. I was happy to not have puked on the Good Doctor.

After the bleeding and fondling, we were sworn in. Immediately afterward, we were told there was a bus leaving in an hour. Any individual not on it would be charged with U.A.

Unauthorized Absence is a violation of the Uniform Code of Military Justice. I was officially a squid. I had walked into the recruiter's office and in one week, inclusive of obtaining a GED, I had become a squid. I would be fed for the next three years, minimum.

I got on the bus.

I couldn't believe they had fallen for it.

Boot

I was too inexperienced to know it at the time, but boot camp employs the classic brainwashing techniques. I don't know about the other services, but in regular old Navy boot camp, the brainwashing isn't about Mother and Country. They drilled us on mostly the hierarchy and all the funny stuff the Navy calls things. Okay, there's team work and all o' that, too, I guess. Like I said, it's the classic "tear a person down and then build them back as you would want them" deal.

We had arrived at the Navy boot camp in San Diego (not near the blood bank or Servicemen's Club), and were waiting in yet another line. I know it was still early in the process because I was in my civilian clothes. I was standing in an outdoor hallway against the wall with my leg cocked and the bottom of my boot on the wall. I saw him coming: some old guy in a light brown uniform. He had locked up on me and was charging.

Shit-oh-dear.

"What the fuck are you doing, recruit?"

My foot slid down the wall as I'm shaking my head at this cat.

What the hell?

"Don't you ever put the sole of your boot on my fucking bulkhead, you fucking worm."

"Uh, yeah, man. Okay."

"You fucking shithead! It's 'yes sir.'

"'Yes sir, *Chief!*' That's the proper response!"

WOW!

"Yes sir, Chief, sir!"

After you got your utilities (clothes), they had you box your civilian clothes and send them home. You are allowed to keep your wallet, wedding ring, and one religious medallion. Everything else goes.

We got to sleep in our new barracks accommodations at about 2:00 in the morning. At 4:00 in the morning some bastards tossed the shit cans down the aisles and started screaming for us worms to get up. As I said: classic brainwashing, the shock part and all.

We got dressed, fell in, and went to breakfast. They fed you three times a day in boot camp. Three times a day, every day! I figured I could work with the brainwashing thing.

The first day was all about learning how to march. It's not like the Navy marches much, but everywhere you go in boot camp, you march. If there are two or fewer of you, you run. We learned how to march going over to the PX.

Sorta.

At the PX we picked up toiletries, stationery and smokes. Our Company Commander ordered us all to buy Dial soap. We would all smell the same. I still use Dial to this day.

Learning to march, at least better than we did on our PX trip, was the main part of the first week or so of training. We would go out on the grinder and march for hours.

The "grinder" is what we called a large asphalted area. Imagine a Sears parking lot without curbs or light posts. There were many seagulls. They would fight over the puke heaved upon the grinder. They were called "grinder pigeons."

You could tell all of the guys who had been longhairs before hitting the barber shop. After the first two days the tops of their ears were terribly fried.

Everything was about inspections. When you mustered (fell in) in the morning, you and your uniform were inspected.

I had never shaved in my life. The Company Commander (CC) detected fuzz on my cheek. The next morning I almost took my upper lip off with a razor. The bitch was I didn't have time for all of that bleeding. I still have the scar.

We were taught how to fold our clothes. Now, I'm not taking about just "folding." I mean folding so that every goddamned pair of drawers in the whole barracks was folded exactly like another. And I mean every piece of clothing in the locker AND placed in exactly the same spot in each locker. The same with the rack (formerly called a bed). Each and every one, exactly the same.

They would tear the lockers apart doing the inspection, spreading the contents. Maybe that's why they had us stencil our names on everything. Any small discrepancy would earn an individual a "hit." So many hits would earn a Marching Party.

A Marching Party was nothing more than a couple of hours of calisthenics out on the grinder. Pushups, sit-ups, leg lifts… that sort of stuff. The real bitch was being out there in the night while the rest of the company wrote letters and listened to the radio after cleaning the barracks.

I know because I did one, and they weren't *my* hits. I was surprised when I was getting ready to catch a shower and my name was read off.

Bullshit.

I knew it was bullshit. I looked at the clipboard and there was Kennedy, James P. with eight hits. Below was Kennedy, Stan with two. Stan was a fuck-up.

I walked over to Stan's rack.

"Motherfucker, those are your hits and you damn well know it. Go over and tell him those are yours."

The son of a bitch started crying on me.

"Man, I've done a Party for the last four nights. I can't do another one tonight. I can't… I can't.

"Please!"

Fuck it.

I gave him one.

One night at mail call I was called to the CC's office. I pounded on the doorjamb and sounded off. I was then granted permission to enter. "This is for you," said the Company Commander. He handed it to me and said, "Open it."

The return address was Collette's. It was obvious the envelope contained three soft, cylindrical objects. Again, I was too naïve to know that I could have simply refused to accept it. I opened it. Collette had sent me three cigarettes.

Cigarettes... whew.

It turned out the Company Commander was a drunk. We weren't a sterling group ourselves. It showed. People noticed.

I happened to be on the barracks fire watch when Salt and Pepper showed up. Salt and Pepper are what they call the trouble-shooters. They straighten out fucked-up companies. The name was derived from the black and white shoulder cords they wore.

They were mean bastards.

I sounded off, "Airman Recruit Kennedy, the time is (whatever), please identify yourself."

S & P responded, "You are relieved of your watch, recruit."

Ah, crap.

They had us lie beside our racks, on our backs and we began "good morning darlings." You know the exercise: feet up six inches, hold, spread, hold, back, hold, down; on their count. The "holds" were quite long. Rinse and repeat.

It was hilarious. Guys were screaming in pain and crying. The troubleshooters were asking us who the fuck-ups were. Kids were yelling out names. The same names, mostly.

Thankfully, they got the right Kennedy.

I was cheating. I could see what direction the two mean bastards were facing from under my rack. My legs were on the ground when they were looking the other way. Apparently I screwed up and got out of count.

Here came trouble. He put his boot in the middle of my chest, with a substantial amount of his weight and asked, "What the fuck makes you so special, recruit?"

Only, like, yelling, as you've seen in the flicks. I hadn't a clue what he was talking about. I looked under the rack over at Bob for some support. Bob was trying to control his laughter.

Fuck you, Bob.

We never saw our old CC again. They brought us another one. We were threatened with the Black Flag. When a company flew the Black Flag, its forward progress stopped. After flying the flag for a week, nine weeks of boot camp became ten.

Bad deal, that black flag.

Our new CC got us whipped into shape though. Hell, he made me the Fifth Squad Leader so you know he had to've had his shit together.

I did well in boot camp. I kept thinking that thousands of guys passed through there every year. I was just another one.

After a few weeks, class training became more prevalent than physical. We would cross a bridge spanning an estuary almost daily going to the classrooms. During one pass the CC pointed out that the water was too shallow to dive into. He said that tossing a rain coat over the barbed wire fence was a better way to go. I couldn't fathom why a person would want to escape. Hell, I had three good reasons to stay: breakfast, lunch and dinner.

A real kicker was a class that I attended that explained the psychological methods that were being employed in our training.

Yeah, no shit, the Navy has a class that explains the why and how of their fucking with your head.

I found it amazing.

The chow line consists of a group of men five abreast and many long. You stand at what we called "nut to butt." That is, I was breathing on the man's neck in front of me. A person can fall asleep and be held up by those on four sides of him. I know. I've taken cat naps that way. I was inboard one day, against the bulkhead, and spied a piece of graffiti. Someone had scrawled, "I am a worm." I did pushups because I couldn't contain my laughter. I had temporarily lost it. I still think it was funny as hell.

Hey! You weren't there, man!

On our last barracks inspection, we got three hits. One for each pot seed they found behind a toilet. The damned weed had been full of 'em. I *thought* I'd found 'em all.

I graduated from boot camp, went home and fucked Collette. Bob went home and got married. I was an usher. We both looked fine in our new Navy dress uniforms.

I wore my "winter blues" a total of three times. The first was during boot camp graduation. The second was the wedding. The last was a dress inspection aboard ship. I maintained the same tie knot from boot. I still don't know how to knot a tie. I'm quite alright with that.

I didn't see Bob again until after I was out. The buddy system is for boot only. It doesn't apply to your first duty station. He told me he spent all of his time in some warehouse in San Diego. His bride would be taken by cancer soon after his separation from the Navy.

They'll let you go a few days in the hole on your leave out of boot camp, as I hadn't yet earned the five days or so I had taken. I hung out a bit, sporting my new squidly look and yucking it up. The drinking age had changed in Arizona to eighteen. Pop and I decided we'd hit a few bars in celebration of my new employment. I twisted a doobie and dropped it in my cigarette pack. I figured if I had a chance to get away, maybe I'd have me a hit or two.

We were going from one country dive to another, in the cab of his ol' Chevy Apache pickup. It was dark. I thought I'd have me a smoke, so I lit one.

Oops.

Yeah. No shit. It was that damned joint. What to do? I mean. It's obviously too late to do anything. There's reefer smoke in the cab. I cracked the window and took a big hit. From the driver's seat I heard, "Sniff, sniff.

"Is that that damned weed, Jim?"

"Uh, yeah."

"Let me have that damned thing."

I thought he was going to toss it out of the window, but instead he took a hit. We smoked the joint on the way to the next bar. While we were waiting on a pool table he tells me, "I don't know about that shit, Jimbo.

"I'm not normally as drunk as I am now with only this many beers."

I'd smoke another joint with Pop twenty years later.

I proposed to Collette and then split from Yuma to some sort of Airman School. I inadvertently left my dog tags hanging on her bedroom door knob. I never saw them again. Basically, the school was two weeks of "This is an airplane.

"This is an aircraft carrier flight deck."

One thing that did stick with me was some of the training videos. When shit would hit the fan, men had a tendency to turn and run. Whether it was, a crash or a wire break, they ran. Most of those guys took it in the back and were maimed or killed.

I got orders for the *USS America* CV66, home ported out of Norfolk, Virginia.

I told myself to never turn my back and run.

WELCOME ABOARD

At the time, the *America* wasn't in Norfolk. It was in the ship-yards at Portsmouth, Virginia. I walked up the gang plank to the afterbrow, located on a lowered elevator three, saluted the Ensign, then saluted the Petty Officer of the Watch and sounded off, "Request permission to come aboard."

The afterbrow is the gangplank that enlisted sailors use to come and go. "Os" (officers) use the front door, known as the quarterdeck.

It didn't quite work that way.

My military I.D. didn't have the ship's sticker on it. All I had was my orders to verify that I was where I was supposed to be. Also, the fact that I was standing there in my winter blues, freezing my ass in the November snow, undoubtedly clued the First Class that I was a boot reporting aboard.

"Let me see your orders."

After a brief examination he turned to the messenger of the watch and had him escort me to the V-2 office. I had been ordered to the Air Department, V-2 division. Planes, remember?

I was guaranteed "something" to do with aviation. I was amazed when I looked into the hangar bay. I was more amazed as we worked our way down the ladders and through the passageways. I don't know that it was a culture shock but it damn sure was an environmental shock. I have tried to explain to people what the interior of a Naval vessel is like. I don't know that I've ever done so with any success.

I suppose I can give it one more shot.

Imagine, if you will, a cave made of welded steel—or maybe a mine would make a better analogy. A mine made of steel. A mine, only because of all the piping and wiring that's strung overhead. Though the deck beneath your feet is (most likely) covered in tile, you know it's steel under the tile. The bulkheads (walls) are steel. The overhead (ceiling) is steel.

You know the overhead is the underside of the deck above. As you travel down passageways you step through frames. Frames are the structural components (bulkheads) that run athwartship.

At every frame crossing the passageway, there is an oval for a person to step though. As you move from deck to deck you pass through these hatches (doors). It's a steel fucking cave, man. Once a few feet beyond the weather deck (the outside), should the light go out (There's emergency light. Without that, okay?), you would not be able to see your hand in front of anything.

Nah.

Now that I think on it some… imagine a steel hive. That's a better description. From here on wherever I've written "cave" think "hive," okay? It'll save me a shitload of editing. Thanks, man.

The messenger of the watch dumped me at the V-2 office, on the 01 level. Or was it the 02? What the hell is the level below the hangar bay? It was that one. The same level as the mess decks.

On a ship, a carrier anyway, all levels above the water line begin with "0". Anything below is without the "0", beginning with One. I'd've never found it on my own, the space that was the V-2 office. I wandered in and came to a desk. There was an E-3 sitting behind it. He looked up and ordered,

"Pop to! Sound off!"

I dropped my sea bag, went to attention and responded, "Airman Apprentice Kennedy, reporting as ordered."

I left off the "Sir." I mean, dude was an E-3.

A Lieutenant walked out of an adjoining office, said, "Goddamnit! I told you to quit fuckin' with the boots! Find him a fuckin' rack. We'll process him tomorrow."

My rack was up forward, on the same level.

At the time I reported aboard, this particular steel cave wasn't being heated. This particular steel cave didn't have hot water either. This was November, in Virginia. It was fucking cold in the bowels of the cave. Really, really, fucking cold. I'm pretty sure they were still feeding us hot food though. They always fed us hot food.

I think.

Hmm, there might be a memory there I'm repressing. This whole deal was about food, remember?

It didn't last long, the no heat. Not more than three or four days. Those days were a bitch though. I had a life changing experience in those three or four days. I would go to the head and take the ultimate "Navy shower." A splash of water on the important parts. A bit of soap and then a rinse. The water was freezing. I would run back to my rack and wrap up in my Navy-issued wool blanket and wait for the shaking to subside before getting dressed.

I ran back to my rack once and some son of a bitch had stolen my blanket.

Gone. It was fucking gone.

Yeah, it was cold enough that some son of a bitch would steal another man's blanket. I've had a hard-on for thieves since. I don't know if "irony" is the right word. It gets abused a lot. I don't believe in karma.

Call it what you want.

The theft did something to my whole conception of "theft." Fuckin' thieves—I hate 'em. I haven't stolen a damned thing since that day. Not. A. Fucking. Thing. Okay, so I still owe that guy for the kilo of weed back in '83, but that's different, right?

I met Fried Fred in the "holding pen." Fred was out of Billings, Montana. His dad was in the tire business there.

It was the August after his graduation from high school that Fred had decided to enlist. The summer party was over and the snows were coming. Fred had heard that if you joined the Navy you could travel the world. To Fred, that equated to partying the world over and sampling the drugs therein. They called him that because his physical attributes were about those of Fred Flintstone. Well, except for the red hair. Imagine a stoned, red headed, Fred Flintstone. Bingo.

Two cats that I had gone to boot with were ordered to the *America*, too: Mike Nova and Ritchie. I don't recall Ritchie's first name. Fred and Nova were going to the V-1 division.

V-1 handles the aircraft on the flight deck. Ritchie might have been a BT, Engineman or something. I don't think he was an Airedale. I don't recall ever seeing him with a flight deck jersey on. He would end up getting quit/fired from the Navy.

V-1, 2, 3 and 4 Divisions are sometimes called Black Shoe Airedales. I think it was back in WW II that Naval aviators first wore brown shoes. The rest of the Navy wore black. I've probably got that twisted, but somethin' like that.

"Airedale" denotes a squid that works with aircraft, not ships. In our case, we transitioned aircraft from here to there. That could be from one end of the deck to another, from the deck to air, from the air to deck, or the handling of the fuel to accomplish any of the above.

Aa-aanyway, the "V" divisions were ship's company. We were part of the crew, not like some squadron puke who came to visit from time to time. Squadron pukes didn't live in steel caves without heat when there was snow on the ground. They lived in base housing at places like Whidbey Island.

So I went back to the V-2 office and they asked me if I wanted to go to the Cats or the Gear. I knew what the Cats were; some dude pushed a button, and the result was an airplane flung off of the end of the deck.

Whoopie!

When he said "Gear," I imagined this great big fucking gear. You know? A disk of toothed metal that meshed with another—a gear, man. "Gear" invoked machinery. I'm a machinery kind of guy.

"I'll take the Gear."

Of course, that would be the Arresting Gear: the men and equipment that bring aircraft to a stop in a relatively short distance. I ended up with the coolest fucking job I've ever had. Also, I believe it's one of the most dangerous jobs on the planet.

Well, that's what they used to say before the crab fishermen got their own TV show, anyway.

We used to go to a joint in downtown Norfolk called Bunny's Trade Winds. There were a couple of pool tables, and if you made it on the right night of the week, there might even be a semi-naked, semi-pro dancer wiggling on a small stage. I spent my first Christmas Eve in the Navy at Bunny's.

One night Ritchie, Nova and I snagged up with three hookers just a short distance from there. Mike was shit faced. I was… uh, okay. I thought Ritchie was okay, but it was always hard to tell with him. We went to one of the gal's places to receive their services. Ritchie had fallen asleep for a few minutes after having concluded the deal. The ship, still in Portsmouth, wasn't that far of a walk. We were halfway there when Ritchie discovered his wallet was empty.

We went back and two huge motherfuckers answered the door. Bummer deal about the contents of Ritchie's wallet. What a dumbfuck anyway, eh?

Rule Number One in whoring: never, ever fall asleep.

When I reported to Arresting Gear I met a colorful cast of people with names like Country, Slim, Stretch, Colorado Ron, C.O., Burnie, Obie, Big Ski, Lil' Ski, Capt. Punk (Punk would later be promoted to Adm.), Fee-Fee…

Others who might have been there already or came later included Stone, Gator, Hairy (his name was Harry but we called him Hairy), Cowboy, Vermin, Rock & Roll, Murf, Rocky...

I was pretty much called "Boot." It was a term of endearment for newly arrived E-2s.

Arresting gear doesn't do anything without an aircraft yanking on its wire. It sits there.

Unless you turn the saltwater coolers on, there's no noise. It doesn't move. It sits there.

Wire, sheaves and cylinders. It's nothing more than machined chunks of metal with liquid and air, held apart with seals, in cylinders weighing in at a total of 43 tons. Sitting there.

Waiting.

The Gear is made of two dampers, port and starboard and an Arresting Gear engine between the two with a shitload of cable run through its sheaves. Imagine a block and tackle arrangement lying on its side, about fifty feet long. One end is fixed, the other end slides on "rails". Between the two is a hydraulic piston/cylinder. As the wire is pulled, the crosshead moves toward the fixed end, pushing the fluid though a variable valve. The valve moves toward closing, things slow down; the valve closes, things stop... hopefully.

The cable plays out of the engine to both port and starboard. On either side, it passes through a sheave damper. From the damper, it goes through the topside sheave and attaches to the Cross Deck Pendant (CDP).

It's the CDP—a steel cable stretching all the way across the landing deck—that takes all of the above-deck abuse. It's easily changed out.

The sheave damper is an enormous shock absorber. That sheave is on the end of another hydraulic set-up. The initial movement of the wire "strokes" the damper rod (max stroke ten feet), taking the brunt of that first shock.

There's a watch station in Arresting Gear called a Sheave Damper Operator. You didn't operate shit. You watched it. Maybe gave it a shot of grease now and again. If something fucked up, you advised the rest of the crew by calling "Foul Deck!" into the sound-powered phones you wore. It wasn't much of a job. It's where the boots started.

I was assigned to Four Port sheave damper. Obie was already the operator there. Obie was still the operator there when I left the ship. Obie liked to huff stuff: Wite-Out, paint, trichloroethylene… you name it. I heard that after I left the *America*, Obie was removed from the vessel in a straitjacket.

The *America* wasn't in the yards long after I reported aboard. We would move to pier 12 in Norfolk after a couple of months. The sand crabs (aka "yard birds", the civilian shipyard workers) were thinning out when I got my "Dear John" letter.

Okay, so it was a phone call. Same shit.

While she was in the yards, the bow of the *America* hung over eight or so phone booths on the dock. Those old booths with the bi-fold doors and the light—the Superman booths. I was sitting in the third booth from the left when Collette told me she thought we should start seeing other people.

To be quite honest, I was more pissed off than hurt. Oh, no one likes rejection. I mean, that's basic emotion stuff, there. Sure that hurt.

Ouch!

The thing is, the only reason I had proposed to her at all was to keep her on the hook while I played squid. You know? That way I'd have a guaranteed piece of ass when I came home on leave.

That was obviously down the shitter.

I hung up and went and got drunk. I don't think I talked to her on the phone ever again. I know I was still living in the bow when we first went to sea—or hell, maybe it was just the move to Norfolk. We were tied to the pier when I hit my rack. When I awoke, we were under power. I looked down the passageway and it was moving up and down along the length of it. I got fucking seasick.

Yeah, no shit. I got seasick on an *aircraft carrier*. Some fucking sailor. It wasn't like I was puking sick, just sick. Nauseous. Green. I hung out in Four Port and listened to Obie make fun of me.

I moved from the bow to Four Port. There wasn't an open rack in the aft V-2 berthing compartment, and walking the length of the damned boat to get from where I slept to where I was really living got to be a pain. I tossed a mattress over a couple of cruise boxes, made a deal with Obie on some locker space and moved in. A cruise box is a folding, sheet metal box. A rack mattress fits perfectly on two of them, lying end-to-end.

I had still not seen the Gear do its thing. It was all still just sitting there. Waiting.

Soon we were headed out for the Atlantic for trials and training. I was in Number Three engine room while it was being functioned. "Functioned" was when the wire was pulled out with a tractor(s). Tractors were what V-1 pulled planes around with. We had an aircraft hook that would mate with the pintle hook on the tractor. You'd drop the hook behind the wire and go like hell in the tractor. It was nothing like a plane, but it made things move.

Cutting through Number Three was the shortcut to my watch station in Four Port. I slowed my step about a quarter of the way through the space. At halfway, I stopped.

I was in awe. I was struck.

I watched the crosshead slowly move toward the fixed end. I watched the cable move through the sheaves. You could feel the weight moving across the deck. There was a bit of growl and rumble.

It was as though the giant was awakening. It was as though it was giving a deep yawn, scrubbing the sleep from its eyes. It was stirring.

I held fast.

Then it appeared to slip back into slumber. The slow movement ceased. The rumble. The wires slackened. I turned toward the port side wondering what Obie was sniffing today.

On deck they had pulled the hook from the tractor. Someone gave the retract signal.

I almost pissed my pants. The previous rumble had become a roar. When the crosshead came to the end of its leash there was a horrendous bang.

Son of a BITCH! It's awake!

They got a big kick out of that. They thought it was funny as hell.

"That was only a retract, Boot. You ain't seen shit yet."

The first trap we took when I was in Four Port, I almost shit my pants.

One of the things that took a bit to get used to is that we were blind under the deck. Not only were we blind, but which wire the plane traps is a roll of the dice. There were two guys on Deck Edge who are in communication with the machinery rooms. One of their responsibilities was to call in the planes. The order (if'n it was a Tomcat) went like this.

"F-14 in the long groove... F-14 in the short groove... F-14 over the ramp... *heads up!*"

At "heads up," you would expect to hear an Arresting Gear engine howl half a second later. Maybe yours.

Maybe not.

The howl of an engine can't be explained. Not really. It's a scream as the fluid is slowly shut down through the valve. The bang, the initial "yank" on the engine and the rumble of the equipment is easier to imagine. The machinery rooms are on the deck above the hangar bay. The mess decks are the next level below the hangar bay. You could plainly hear an engine scream on the mess decks. It was an ear-piercing screech within the machinery space.

So I was a sheave damper operator, apprenticed to a glue sniffer.

We were in port and I was going to hit the beach. The "beach" in squidly terms means to go on liberty. Get off the boat. It hadn't anything to do with sand and surf.

The hatch to Four Port had a chain with a lock on it. Anytime we weren't in the space, we kept it locked. Now that I think on it, we would lock ourselves in at times, too. Looking at the chained and locked hatch, one wouldn't imagine that a sailor might be inside getting stoned.

When I went to catch a shower, I didn't bother to lock up. I haven't the foggiest idea why, especially being's I had left sixty dollars in twenties and two joints sitting out on a cruise box. The joints were sitting on top of the money. After I returned and was in the process of getting dressed, the hatch opened. It was the highest-ranking Master Chief on the ship. This dude was Big Cheese Man. A wheel. He popped his head in.

"Where have you been, Sailor?"

"I grabbed a shower, Chief," I said. "I'm getting ready to hit the beach."

In a panic, I tossed the two doobies behind the damper, into the drip pan.

"You shouldn't leave this space unsecure. You have sixty dollars lying there." He looked concerned for my welfare. "Anyone could have taken it."

"You're right, Chief," I admitted. "I got lazy. I'll keep it locked up in the future."

You realize he had to've moved the joints aside to count the money, don't you? The money had been folded together.

On paydays, Stone, Hairy and I used to split the cost of a motel room for the weekend in Ocean View. Nova might have been there sometimes, too.

Stone and I had gravitated together, for some reason. Opposites attract? I dunno.

Stone had been in his third semester at Bellevue Community College, majoring in video production, when he enlisted in the

Navy. The money for a four-year program was his, then he fucked up, got stoned and drove by the Navy Recruiters office.

Use the "munchies" as an analogy, if you will. He was stoned and looking for something to chew on… an adventure. Yeah, the marketing snagged yet another unsuspecting victim.

"Accelerate your life."

Gator was probably at the motel sporadically. He was married, but things were a bit rocky with them.

We'd always ask for the same room. It had a big window that looked out on the bay. It was cool to watch the weather and water as we got stoned. Heaven knows no one was getting laid.

We sort of used it for a base camp as we barhopped and whatnot. I was introducing Fried Fred to the fold and had invited him out one weekend. We were sitting at the table smoking weed when Fred took a big hit, passed out, fell out of his chair and went into convulsions. I was embarrassed.

Fuckin' Fred…

We were getting ready to head to South America when I got busted. I was still living and working in Four Port when it happened.

The Gear got the word that there was going to be a raid. Apparently, the Gear had become a bit nefarious in the eyes of the Master at Arms.

MAs were the coppers.

The word went out for everyone to clear out their spaces and lockers. Everyone knew there was going to be a "surprise inspection." They waited until immediately after a General Quarters drill to pull us all into the shop—the whole Gear crew. They would take several individuals off and have them open their rack lockers or anything else a person had a lock on. They searched the spaces. All they found was a few seeds.

In a locker in Four Port, as I live and work.

In a locker without a lock on it.

Me and Obie got drug down to the MA shack for questioning. I figured they didn't have shit on us. There was no lock on the locker. No ownership. Anyone had access. They didn't have shit. I told them so. I told 'em to get fucked.

"It's chow time, motherfucker," I said. "I'm hungry and I've had enough of this shit.

"I'm outta here."

The MA told me to empty my pockets and then I was free to go. I had forgotten about that little pipe. That little pipe that I had had plenty of opportunity to get rid of. That little pipe that my fingers had just found, in my left pocket. That little fucking pipe.

When I went back up to the shop after being charged, the fellas were all guffawing about the big bust the MAs had been expecting. They were yucking it up about how the coppers didn't get shit. When I walked through the *door* into the shop (it was a door, not a hatch), Colorado Ron asked, "What about you, Boot Camp?

"How'd that whole bullshit seed thing work out?"

I told my tale of woe. The shop was dead silent for a few seconds. Guy's jaws were kind of hanging. Heads were being shaken side to side, as if in disbelief.

Colorado finally said, "You are a fucking drift. A motherfucking *drift*."

He looked like he couldn't decide if he wanted to laugh or be ill.

"No, Ron," Country said. "Not *a* drift. He's the damned *captain* of all fucking drifts.

"He's *Captain* Fucking Drift."

That was the day Capt. Punk got promoted to Admiral. You couldn't have two captains in the same division.

From that day forward I was known as Cap'n Drift, Drift or CD. I once had a boot ask me, "Drift, what's your first name?"

I'm not sure why one would feel rewarded for being an idiot, but that was the day I was no longer "Boot Camp." I was getting noticed.

I had a name.

I moved my rack to Three Port. Obie was being a bitch over the whole drug bust thing. There was a question about whose seeds they had been, and Obie was getting kind of weird.

I moved my shit.

I started using a hammock for my rack in Three Port, tying one end through a hole that had been cut in the web of an I-beam. That turned out to be a mistake.

I awoke one morning realizing there were two people in the space with me. I was one of those for whom it took a while before they got their shit together. I was still in that process when the context of their conversation began to dawn on me. The hammock rope through the eye beam was being sawn through by the jagged edge.

"Look, there goes another strand. Every time he moves, it cuts another one."

"Should we tell him?"

"No. Let's see if it breaks before he gets up. I've got five bucks that says he bounces."

Holy shit! This thing's going to fall!

I sat up just as the rope at my head gave way. I hit the steel deck flat on my back, bouncing my noggin.

As I laid there trying to find a gulp of air, I heard, "Son of a bitch... but he didn't really bounce."

"You know what I meant. Pay up, motherfucker."

I was still working in Four Port the night the Tomcat hit the ramp. I wasn't down in Four Port but at Deck Edge, actually. It was a trip, man.

We had each done a hit of acid. That would have been me, Obie and the portside sheave damper, Petty Officer Wins. I'm probably spelling his name wrong, but I won't have spell check chasing my ass for the rest of this book if I spell it "Wins." That's the way it sounded, anyway.

Wins popped into the machinery space and asked if I'd like to play a game of chess. He was a freak for chess. Now that I think on it, I suppose it's kind of weird playing a game of chess in a space where a guy yells "heads up!" every now and again and you put your hands over your ears, waiting to see if it'll be you that takes the trap.

The acid thing, not so weird. I told him no, I didn't want to play chess. I wanted to go see what was going on, on deck.

In V-1, they throw you right into the deep end of the pool. They start you out as a Blue Shirt. Being a Blue Shirt has to be one of the most physical jobs on the planet. You carry chocks and chains all shift. The days and nights can be quite long.

Whenever an aircraft is moved, unless it's taxiing under its own power (and even then, sometimes), two guys walk with the main mounts of the plane.

Carrier aircraft have three wheels. There's the two under (or about under) the wings and then the third under the front portion of the fuselage. That front one is called "nose gear." Those under the wings are the "main mounts." The Blue Shirts each carry a chock and normally have tie-down chains hanging over their shoulders. They chock and tie the plane upon the command of the director, or Yellow Shirt.

They do that hour after hour. It's tough fuckin' work, man. I'm tellin' ya.

Nova was a Blue Shirt. He would pop down the port catwalk and dive into Four Port now and again for a quick hit off a joint. He'd be covered in grime. He said it was the coolest thing he had ever done, being a Blue Shirt. Nova worked on the flight deck of an *aircraft carrier.*

Fred, too, would speak of his day's activities on the deck. He wasn't quite as exuberant as Nova, but he also thought it was pretty fuckin' cool.

I didn't want to just be an apprentice to a paint huffer. I wanted to see the action on deck. In the sheave damper machinery space, you could hear the planes' landing gear hit. Hell, you could hear their engines. Obviously, if they trapped your wire, you saw the machine work, the cable playing. I wanted to go see the fish on the end of the line.

The action.

Hanging out with Obie and playing chess with Wins sucked. That, undoubtedly, contributed to my resorting to dropping acid to shake things up.

I don't know if it was just because he was tripping or that he commiserated (both?), but Wins said he'd take me on deck. We stopped at the shop and picked up some spare topside gear. That consisted of a cranial helmet with attached sound attenuators, goggles, and a "float coat" (an inflatable vest in the event you went over the side). We suited up and walked down the passageway to the catwalk, up the ladder, and onto the flight deck. He had me hold back while he conferred with Colorado Ron, the Topside Petty Officer. Wins waved me on and I followed him to Deck Edge.

Have I mentioned this was at night?

There were basically six Arresting Gear watch stations on the flight deck. There was the Topside PO with his Safety. He stood back around where the Three Wire emerged from the deck on the starboard side. Topside, the Topside PO was head cheese for Gear after the Arresting Gear Officer.

The Topside PO stood by the wires so that he could run out and make a quick inspection of the CDP in the event of a hook skip or a spit. Sometimes a hook would barely snag the wire, spit it out and go on to engage the next.

Had it fucked up the wire?

The Topside PO (with permission from the Gear Officer) would run out onto the landing area and inspect the wire. Due to the direction of the hook impact, he had to do that with his back to the fantail. That would be the same fantail that another aircraft was approaching. The Safety stood facing the ramp, calling out the plane's distance, to let him know if it was on final approach and hadn't gotten back on the power.

The Topside PO wore what we called a "mouse." He had a mic and speakers installed in his helmet. He could speak to the Air Boss or anyone else on the deck wearing the mouse, such as the Gear Officer.

There was also the LSO platform. You've seen that on the education channels; the pilots that talk in the birds? LSO stood for "Landing Systems" or "Landing Signaling" (or some such landing shit) "Officer." There was a gear dude on the platform, too. He'd visually identify aircraft three planes back and report his "spots" to Primary.

It sounded like this:

"Primary, LSO."

"Go, LSO."

"Spot one, F-14 Tomcat. Spot two, F-14 Tomcat. Spot three, A-7 Corsair."

"Roger that, Tomcat one and two. A-7 spot three."

And then Primary would tell Engines and Lens to set for the Tommy, if Primary hadn't done so already. Sometimes Punk would take it on himself to set up the first plane in a recovery. Hell, from the tower he had a better view than from the deck. The lens system is set for each different aircraft, too, just like the

Engines. It's a fresnel system. Got a minute? I'll briefly explain. No, really. It'll just take a few seconds.

The jockeys would fly in on a given pattern. They had read the manual on carrier landings. The manual told them they got to cheat; they'd have the LSO chatting them up with instructions and they'd have a visual cue. That visual is a "light tree" mounted on the port side of the ship. The tree is a set of lights in a sort of a cross laid over at 90 degrees arrangment, the horizontal arms being longer than the vertical.

That aircraft's position, relative to the three wire and the deck, is represented on that tree -- the "Meat Ball." The pilot knows if he's high, low, port or starboard by the lights lit on the tree.

The jockey flies (falls?), he listens to the LSO, he watches the lights. He can't see the flight deck -- his aircraft being in a nose up attitude. He'd watch the lights and drop his plane in, hoping to keep the light at the intersection of the arms lit.

Yeah. He couldn't see the deck... Not until he was over the top of it.

Different planes, different angles of attack. The lens was set for aircraft just like the Engines.

Primary would get word that both were set. He would pass word to gear dude on the "platform."

At that point he would call out, "Gear, lens set F-14, Tomcat. Gear down. Hook down. Clear deck."

Unless that pesky Topside PO and his sidekick the Safety were still out there looking at wires, in which case he would call "foul deck" and the Safety would start getting nervous.

Another station was the Hook Runner. I'll go into detail on that position a bit later... great detail.

We'll move on to Deck Edge.

Deck Edge was a two-man position. It was called Deck Edge because… uh, it's on the edge of the deck? It's a starboard, aft, catwalk-like platform with handles and levers and stuff, mounted to the bulkhead. Standing on Deck Edge, the flight deck hit about nipple level.

These guys wore sound-powered phone sets in their helmets. They were in communication with Primary and all of the equipment operators. Between the two of them, they called in the planes to the blind bastards below, and informed the Gear Officer of the weight settings and that the previously retracted engine was back in "battery" (i.e. ready for the next bird).

Because it was located in a rather precarious spot, Deck Edge had an emergency chute. The idea was that if a landing aircraft was terribly fucked up and was about to put it in your lap, you had a place to go.

Sorta.

It was a slide that dropped one weather deck down. There was a fireman's pole arrangement in the center of it. Later, I would find out it was great fun to push your buddy down the chute. That was right up there with pulling the inflation cord on his float coat.

So off we went to Deck Edge. I was told to stay back out of the way and simply observe.

Observe? That's not the right word.

Does a person "observe" dragons? Does a person "observe" the fact that their senses are overwhelmed? Does a person stand outside himself and "observe" a train wreck? There, but apart, too? Maybe that's why I didn't immediately react. I was merely an observer. Dissociated from reality.

Trippin', man.

At night, the aircraft approached differently than during the day. At night, they lined up from miles back to make a run for the deck. The variously colored identifying lights looked like jewels strung out in the sky behind the ship. As the lead lights sharpened, you could begin to discern subtle movements. As it got into the short groove, you could hear the engine(s) whine, lights still the only thing visible.

It came over the ramp into the subdued lighting and you could now hear the roar. The phantom, the ghost, apparition, had appeared... and it was *pissed*. Its hook would strike the deck, sending up a rooster tail of sparks. The hook engaged a wire, and sparks flew from the topside sheaves as the purchase cable played out. With the aircraft now forward, you could watch the fire shut down in its exhaust, the beast captured. And then it was almost quiet. The only sound was a lone aircraft. Forward. Slowly taxiing.

And now another one coming.

On acid, it was *really*, really... I mean, like, really cool.

Plane crashes were a trip, too—even if you weren't tripping. I've had 'em both ways.

Having no experience whatsoever on the flight deck, I had no idea how to tell a good approach from bad. Besides, all of those sparks really had me enthralled. Spellbound.

I was a boot! What do you expect?

An F-14 was in the short groove. I was already getting the I.D. thing down by the location and color of the lights.

Then the fellas disappeared down the emergency chute.

Okay, we need to do the time dilation thing here for a few paragraphs. That time thing where a second is like a minute. That's dilation, right? Or am I going the wrong way?

Time slowed. That's what I mean.

The F-14 came in low and hit the round-down. The round-down is a sloped section at the very aft of the flight deck. Hold your hand in front of you with about 20 degrees slope from horizontal and imagine flying an F-14 fighter into it at 125 knots.

Yeah, he was a *little* low.

The plane exploded. Then the damned thing proceeded to go ahead and come up on—and then rapidly along—the angle deck.

Here it comes.

I was frozen. I don't know that it was so much of a panic. I don't recall a feeling of panic. It was more like stunned. A bit of shock, maybe. When I felt the heat from the fire and the pieces of non-skid deck coating hit my face, I managed to get my knees to buckle. The plane was on fire from the cockpit back, and had traveled clear past the Island.

"The Island" is what we called the superstructure above the flight deck. I caught sight of a main mount bouncing toward the general vicinity of the Topside PO's spot as I fell down the chute.

What a fuckin' trip, man.

We got lucky that night. I don't believe in "luck," actually. It's just a saying.

No one died. The aircrew punched out of the aircraft and were recovered. The plane simply slid clear off the end of the angle deck.

Scratch one F-14.

The Topside PO told stories about how close the debris had come to taking him out. For days.

That night, I decided I would work on the flight deck. I had to. I didn't have a choice. I had heard the Siren song, you see?

Afterward, Wins beat me again in another game of chess.

POTPOURRI

They started checking me out on Number Two Engine.

I was scheduled for Captain's Mast from back when I had forgotten about that little gem in my pocket.

Nova got himself smashed between the back of the seat in a tractor and the elevator of an F-14.

He had fallen asleep sitting in the tractor while the rest of V-1 was moving aircraft around on the deck. A Director was spotting an F-14 being towed on a bar behind another tractor. He was backing the plane into the spot. The Director couldn't see Mike in his peripheral vision as he watched the horizontal stabilizer just clear over the tractor's hood. The elevator contacted Mike at or just below the sternum.

It crushed him.

I found out later that Mike made it. I certainly didn't think he would when I visited him in Sick Bay. He was unconscious. There were tubes pushing stuff in and tubes sucking stuff out.

His torso was uncovered. It was black from his collar bones to his waist. Not black and blue.

Black.

That was the last time I saw Mike. I figured I was looking at a dead man.

We had set out on a South American cruise June 10th of '77 when I went to Mast. It was after we had left St. Thomas in the Virgin Islands, but before we hit the South American ports.

I enjoyed St. Thomas. It's one of the few places we visited that I wouldn't mind returning to. At Mast, I got fined half a month's pay for two months, a suspended bust (I kept E-2) and 30 days restriction to the ship.

A fellow V-2 crew mate and I took up Frisbee. Pat was from the Cats and was on restriction himself. The first lesson we learned was you don't play Frisbee on the flight deck.

After obtaining another Frisbee, we moved to the hangar bay. Another advantage to that is the Restricted Man's Musters are held in the hangar bay, four times a day when in port. Muster is like a roll call. It can go bad for ya if you miss one or more.

You cross the equator going down that-a-way. I went through the super secret ritual that everyone's seen on the Discovery Channel, and became a Shellback. There was a guy in the Gear that refused to play the game, yet wanted his certificate. We got to the paperwork before the first class and tossed his over the side.

Fuckin' pussy.

Speaking of rituals, there was also Initiation. The Cats and the Gear each had their own. I had heard that just previously to my reporting aboard, some dudes in the Cats got in a jam for shoving a broom handle up some guy's ass. I had heard a rumor of a grease gun up the butt in the Gear. Thankfully, these practices were no longer employed when I arrived. Frankly I hadn't any, uh, "hard" evidence that any of that had ever happened. I have to wonder if it wasn't all about putting the *fear* into the boots.

We had the Dogpile.

Actually, it was an honor to be the recipient of said pile. That meant you had been accepted as a Gear Rat. After the pile, you were one of the fellas. The prospective recipient was expected to attempt to fight his way out of the shop when he realized what was about to happen. The harder he fought, the better.

I left a few guys a bit sore when my number came up. I almost made it through the door, even. I was right there when Admiral Punk popped through the hatch in the passageway and startled me. That one second of hesitation was all it took—that and Punk slamming me in the chest, driving me backward.

Cowboy and I broke a couple of Vermin's ribs in a Dogpile. It wasn't on purpose. Cowboy was from Wyoming or one of those cowboy places. Later, while we were in the Mediterranean, I'd walk into the shop to find him rosining up a bull rope. He had it tied off to the overhead. He'd heard a fella could pay to ride a bull in Rota, Spain.

Cowboy and I were buddies. We had elected ourselves to be the "take 'em out" guys in a Dogpile. He would hit 'em high, I would hit 'em low. Down we would go. *Boom.* Just like that. They never had a chance.

So it was Vermin that was getting piled.

If a guy had any situational awareness at all, he'd realize that the majority of the crew—about 30 guys—was all in the shop at once.

Did someone call a meeting?

Second, he'd see guys moving chairs and such away from the center of the space. The center of the space that was empty, where a wire spool table should have been.

Cowboy and I keyed on their eyes as the cue for when to strike. When they got big, then *bang*, baby!

We took 'em out.

Obviously, that put the two of us at the bottom of the pile along with the victim. We didn't care. We thought it was a blast.

Cowboy and I were on the deck lying with our faces somewhat close. The guys were piling on. Vermin's rib cage was exposed. I saw the look in Cowboy's face and thought I'd beat him to the punch, as it were. Both of our fists impacted poor old Vermin, side by side. Cracked a couple of 'em, we did.

Oops.

And then there was the coffee pot incident. It was a full-house hundred-potter. The pile was aggregating close to the bench where the brew was sitting. Somehow, some way, someone snagged the cord as they went to jump the victim of the moment. The whole contents of the pot came down upon the crew. Burnie ended up down at Sick Bay with third degree scalding.

He combed flesh from his scalp for two weeks.

I don't recall exactly what the deal was, but I seem to remember we were carrier-qualifying the Brazilians. Why that would happen, I haven't the foggiest. Does Brazil even have aircraft carriers?

Were we expecting their planes to be running carrier operations with our aircraft?

Hell, I don't know. They sure liked to trap short. I do know that.

One and Two Arresting Gear engines lived in the same machinery space. The operator's end of One was starboard. The operator's end of Two was port. The fifty foot-long machines lay athwartships. Port to starboard, vice versa.

There was a door—not a hatch!—on each end that opened to the port and starboard Zero Three Passageway on the deck below the flight deck. Those passageways ran nearly the length of the ship, on that deck.

Gator was running Number One. I was the Number Two operator, having been successfully trained by my chemical-huffing predecessor.

It didn't take long. I'm a quick study. Hell, I could make weight settings (each type of aircraft has a different setting) with my foot while sitting on a stool. That would be with that door closed, of course.

I don't know what started the grease gun fight. The machines have a pneumatically operated, automatic lubrication system, but there's the handheld, too. It's the same can you might see in any automotive lube shop. I didn't know what pressure *they* ran, but *our* guns would shoot a string of grease sixty feet or more, from door to door across the machinery space.

It made a fucking mess.

The short-trapping Brazilians were working the shit out of One and Two. Three and Four were hardly getting any hits. I finally had to have the topside crew pull my CDP. Two was too hot to safely operate. The coolers were going. I'd dumped all the fluid that was allowed. She was cooking. No CDP, no traps.

Those Brazilians sure loved flirting with the fantail. No one had seen anything like it.

It was the second day lying off of Rio De Janeiro that I jumped ship. I had been looking at Rio through a pair of binoculars in between restricted man's musters and Frisbee. There was Sugar Loaf, the big-assed Christ statue. I could see shacks built under a bridge. Less than a quarter mile away there were skyscraper condominiums. There was a white beach there. It was covered with scantily clad young women.

I talked Jim Jenner into loaning me his I.D. card. Jim and I were similar in build and facial structure. A quick glance at the photo on the I.D. and a person wouldn't suspect. You've got to have the card both to leave and get back on the ship. The MAs hold your card while you're restricted. They give it back at your last muster. I was going to miss a few musters and have hell to pay.

Did I mention that was Rio out there? I'd pay hell with interest. Gladly.

I spent the day lying on a bamboo mat spread upon the white sand drinking International beer. I was appalled to observe that the majority of the young, scantily clad young women had more hair in their armpits than I had on my head.

Shocked.

I tried not to gawk.

For the musters I missed, Hell extracted another hundred dollars and another ten days restriction, along with extra duty. I thought it a small price. Actually, I got lucky.

"Lucky" is just an idiom of convenience, remember.

When the Captain asked the fella before me if he had anything to say, the goofy bastard whipped out his bi-fold wallet and spoke into it.

"Scotty, beam me up."

Great. Just fucking great, and I'm next.

I was standing there, lying my ass off about why I had missed those musters—and he knew it—when a sailor approached the Captain and somewhat whispered, "Sir, we have an unidentified submarine off of the starboard bow."

The gavel fell and Mast was over. It could have gone much worse for me.

I doubt they ever discovered if it was friend or foe. Subs are like that. They don't care to chat it up with *anyone*. They hide. Now you see me… now you don't.

I certainly hope it was one of ours. I'd hate to be beholden to *them*.

Whenever we pulled out of port, man overboard drills were common. I think it served two purposes, the drill for the drill's sake and to ensure we left with the same number of squids we arrived with.

Sometimes they would throw "Oscar" overboard to see if a watch or someone would spot the floating dummy. It wasn't unusual for them to yank a couple of guys from their respective departments to see if they would be missing from the muster.

During a man overboard drill, the muster is supposed to be by sight only. If someone says Joe Blow is in the head sitting on the crapper, then the person taking the muster either waits for him or goes to the head to physically confirm Joe Blow is indeed on the vessel.

As per SOP, we had a drill pulling out of Rio. The number of squids was as it should be. That night, someone reported a man overboard. They had seen a float coat or something in the water. One individual came up missing. The helos searched and found nothing but a piece of clothing.

Bummer deal.

The guy's family was notified that their son had been lost at sea.

The story I heard was the son of a bitch walked into his parents' house about a week later. It had been a scam. Dude was never on the ship when we left port. Apparently, a co-conspirator had somehow covered for him during the man overboard drill (not supposed to happen; heads should've rolled), then tossed something over the side later that evening. Dude came up missing during *that* muster, indicating it must have been him that went into the water.

I heard his old man beat the shit out of him and called the cops.

I took to scratching "CD" in the bottom, same corner, of the food trays on the mess decks. It came to me one day while I was standing there in line, tray in hand, waiting to get to the food troughs. I wondered how many times I might have held that same tray, so I started marking them with my pocket knife. It wasn't long before I started finding my mark. I would then scribe a slash. When I left I know of one tray that was marked at eight.

The thing is, though, my study group was compromised.

The whole crew knew what I was doing. Have you noticed the whole crew always knew about everything? I was standing there and the fucking boot behind me whipped out his knife and struck a line beside my initials, on his tray.

"What are you doing?"

"I got a 'CD' tray." He grinned. "I'm marking it."

"No, you stupid son of a bitch. No one scribes them but me.

"You're fucking up my program!"

The dick started making his own mark in another corner. There wasn't much I could say about that. Not too much, anyway.

Boots, I tell ya...

There were a couple of other things I did while standing in the chow line, in an effort to minimize the reality of standing in a line in order to eat.

To this day I have a thing about lines. There have been movies or other events that I've declined to attend simply because of the line.

It wasn't often, but there were times when the chow line would extend clear into the hangar bay. There were a few instances when we realized that we'd never make it to the next go, so we'd skip the line to the front, grab some bread, and make choke-and-slides (i.e. peanut butter and butter sandwiches) and call it good.

I've got a real thing about fucking lines.

One stunt I devised was what I called the "Big Bang." Normally you'd shuffle along a bit at a time. With the Big Bang I wouldn't proceed. I'd stand and wait until fifteen feet or so was between me and the next guy, and then I'd close the gap, *bang*, just like that. For the guys beyond eyesight, it had to have made them wonder. Possibly even given them some sort of false hope, after standing there wondering what the deal was.

What? You think that's being mean? Teasing a bit, maybe, but not actually mean.

"Mean" was more like waiting until I was below decks, where the line would run for thirty feet or better down the passageway, stepping out and yelling, "Hey, *Boot Camp!*" Three or four guys would instinctively turn to respond. Gotcha!

Heh.

You'd hear guys laughing at them. That was mean.

I forgot to mention the motorcycle I had bought from Spit while we were still in Norfolk. I think I gave him a couple of hundred bucks for it a few months before we left for points south. It was some sort of Yamaha that had been crashed, tweaked and twisted. It had an over-length front end with no neck work (I call it "pogo sticking"). It had an in-date base sticker stuck to its down tube.

We rode that fucker to the bars in Virginia Beach from pier 12, many a night. It was so twisted that the expansion joints in the highway would have it jumping in the air and trying to go sideways at 60 mph.

One night Stone, or Fred, or Gator (one of 'em, I'm pretty sure) and I were headed back to the boat from an evening of Virginia Beach carousing. I had a lit cigarette in my hand right when we hit the freeway back to Norfolk. I let it go while my hand was still on the throttle grip (yeah, I know—I don't do *that* anymore, either).

Soon after, my passenger—whoever it was—started beating the crap out of me. He was smacking me about my right side.

I looked down to a well-fanned fire. Flames and flaming debris were trailing out behind us. I was on fucking fire. The damned butt had swung around into my jacket pocket and lit it off.

It bummed me, man. That was a decent suede jacket. The burns to my flesh weren't bad. It really trashed my cool jacket, though. The cotton pocket was burned clear out of it.

Then there was the time the throttle cable broke off at the grip. I took the wire and wrapped it over the frame and down to the foot peg, tying it off. A push on the peg meant go. I rode it for quite a while like that. By that time no one would ride with me anymore, so I didn't have to worry about explaining it to them.

There was no key to it. I'd hook up the battery and kick her off. She started most of the time. I got in the habit of pulling the battery out when I left it at the pier or curb. I don't know why. It's not like someone would steal it. Tow it off maybe, but steal it?

I guffaw.

I'd drop the battery into the helmet and then carry the two by the chin strap. I was at the bar one night when I knocked the helmet over, spilling the contents. I took it into the head and ran a shitload of water through it. Still, by the time I got back to the ship the black dye from the liner was running down my face. Holes had burned through the Styrofoam padding.

Over the next few days, some of my hair fell out. Not much.

When I got back from Brazil, five weeks from the day we had left Norfolk, the bike was gone from the pier parking lot. That saved me from having to ride it off of the end of the pier like I had told the fellas I was gonna do.

Upon our return Hairy and Stone got an apartment in Virginia Beach. We ate a lot of acid. We ate a whole *helluva* lot of acid.

We were in a training sequence where we'd go out into the Atlantic and catch airplanes for a week or so, then be in port for a week or so. Our next real deployment was some time off, so Stone and Hairy got a place. It was off Diamond Springs Blvd. I remember because I would get my own place across the street a bit later. Fred was there, Gator was there, and Burnie from time to time. I'm not sure if it was during this whole apartment phase or when I was side cleaning (I'll try to remember to touch on "side cleaning") that I became an alcoholic.

Nah.

Who am I bullshitting? My history with alcohol abuse/use goes way back before adolescence. Other than an ass whoopin' here and there it would be almost another decade before my boozing would get me into real trouble—land me in jail.

But that's another story.

Typically we'd toss down a bunch of those little baby, eight-ounce beers on the way to the boat every morning. It softened the acid hangovers, and/or helped to smooth things over should the previous evening have gone, uh… a little rough.

I mean, you crack open a beer for a fella, handing it to him, it's tough for him to stay pissed. Stone used to get after me for being mean to Gator all of the time—and does to this day. It's not personal. It's just that Gator's so damned easy to be mean to.

Take that time we were tripping and he kept trying to go the bummer route. It might have started with the fireflies out in the back yard. A neighbor bitching at us, or us telling him he needed to maintain… I dunno. He was harshing my gig, man.

So I decided to do away with him.

I handed Gator a mirror. He went to a corner of the apartment and sat on the floor. There wasn't any furniture. He stayed there the rest of the evening. Now and again he would cry out in terror or rave with maniacal laughter, but he didn't move. I looked over once when his sobbing caught my attention. He was stuck "there" for hours.

Stone still says it was a mean thing to do.

One day I paid a bit closer attention to the practice bomb they were using for a door stop. I've no idea how it got from the ship to their entryway. *I* didn't do it, okay?

It was a similar bomb to the Mk 76. A couple of feet long, maybe. Fins on one end, a bulbous nose on the other. There was a hollow tube down the center. A charge rode in the nose. When the bomb made impact, smoke and a bit of flame blew out of the tail as a marker.

So it was just a damned practice bomb. So what?

I noticed this one was still armed. The pin and charge were still in place. I mean, it's not like it would have blown the walls off the apartment, but it could damn well singe your hair. Worse yet, set the place afire.

That was our place, y'know?

There was talk of setting the charge off out back, but I didn't witness it. I wasn't there. I don't know what they did with it, and you can't prove nothin'.

We were going to be at the pier for a couple of weeks, so I decided it would be a good time to take leave. There isn't any airplane catching going on when the ship is tied to the pier. The non-rates are sent TDY (temporary duty). That can be duty driver, in-port fire party, side cleaners… any number of varying jobs. I've done the three I just mentioned.

At that particular time, I think I was side cleaning. Side cleaning is the most fucked-up job I've ever had. It's funny that I was almost killed doing it, too.

Side cleaners chipped and painted the exterior of the ship. Side cleaning was a 0700 to 1530 job, five days a week unless you had duty. Then you went back to your department to pull the after-brow messenger watch or some shit.

Have you ever run a needle gun on a steel plate all damned day?

The needle gun was a diabolical pneumatic device. It was cylindrical, about a foot long and three inches across. With a weight around three to five pounds, holding it in one hand for hours… well, it got heavy.

It was hooked to a huge compressor. On the business end were the "needles." Don't think hypodermic. They were around 3/16 of an inch in diameter. When those were placed against painted steel and the trigger pulled, paint flew. The rattle was so deafening, it drove me to drinking.

Okay, okay! It gave me a reason. We drunks are like that.

At lunch, we would walk down to the "geedunk" (Navy term for snack shack) and grab a bite. You could buy a 24-ounce cup of beer cheaper than a 16-ounce soda pop.

Who the hell wants to run a needle gun on a steel plate all day, dead sober? I sure as hell didn't.

There were times when I would be working up under an elevator in a little cubbyhole. I'd tie the trigger back on the needle gun, wedge it in a corner and take a nap. To anyone listening from the pier, it sounded like I was one needle-gunning son of a bitch.

Yeah, right.

It was from the barge on the port side that I almost pissed my life away.

The starboard was pierside. The port was open water. We were running a snorkel lift off a barge, painting the underside of something or another. We were done having great fun running a guy out over the bay and then slowly immersing the basket so that he had to stand on the top rails to stay dry. The paint buckets were floating around in there, too. I laughed so hard I had to piss.

I reached over and flipped the switch on the base of the lift, giving control of the basket back to the poor swab we'd been having our way with.

I walked across the deck of the barge to piss on the hull of the *America*. Let's call it a symbolic gesture.

I had one hand on my pecker. The other was on the hull, as I leaned forward across the gap between barge and ship. Our securing lines had a lot of slack. The barge began to float away from the ship; the gap widened. I gave a shove with my hand to transfer my weight back to the barge.

I didn't make it.

I let go of my dick and pushed with both hands. I still didn't make it.

The gap had widened further. I fell into the gap. I was between the ship and the barge. I couldn't reach up to the deck of the barge and it was about the same distance, out of harm's way, to my left or right. The barge started floating back. As I was visualizing my head being squashed like a punkin, I grabbed a big breath and dove. Swimming down was the hardest part. It was dark and I had to feel to know when I had cleared the bottom of the barge. I swam along its bottom and popped up on the far side, noggin intact and pants zipped up.

The guys hauled my soaked ass back aboard the barge. I was sent down to sick bay for a series of inoculations due to the bugs living in the water I'd been swimming in.

It really wasn't until we set ourselves adrift that I decided it was time for a break. Someone fucked up and all our lines got released at once. We were out there a good couple hundred yards before a tug came along and pushed us back to the hull of the ship.

Yeah, time for a break.

Leave was granted rather quickly when the ship was tied to the pier with rattle guns chipping paint all the daylong from its hull.

I put in my paperwork and was on a plane a week later.

Leave... and a New Girlfriend

Chaunce and Sis had married. Sis was with child. I was hanging out at their place. Pop and Betty had divorced.

I tried to talk Collette out of a piece of ass, but that didn't work. She did say she'd haul me around town. Yeah, I'm not sure what was up with that, either. I only did it for a day. It took me that long to reconcile myself to the fact she wasn't going to put out.

While she *was* chauffeuring me around, we stopped at 8th Street Market. Betty had gotten a job there as a checker. I grabbed a sixer and went through her line to say "hey."

Betty shot a smug look at Collette and said, "You oughtta drop by my place later.

"Alone, so I can have you all to myself."

She would call me later and say that she was moving to Oklahoma in the next few days and wanted to know if I wanted to ride her... er, along with her. Now you see what I mean about that latent jealousy thing I mentioned earlier?

Truth be told, I'd stood masturbating in the shower on an occasion or two, fantasizing about what that encounter could have been like. Don't tell those dudes Freud or Oedipus about this, okay? We'll just keep it between us.

At the time, even though I was desperately hunting for a piece of tail, screwing my foster mom just seemed too weird. I suppose it's funny how time can change one's perspective. I mean, she was a well-built, attractive woman, only a few years older than I. Pop had married a young one. She's always as she was then when I'm fantasizing...

Oh, never mind. I went with plan B.

There was a gal I had met a couple of years earlier. Her name was Belinda. She was five years older than me. Belinda was best buddies with Chaunce's sister.

That was the original connection.

Maybe I should loop back and give you some background on that. Belinda *is* rather important to the story line.

I met her when Terry was living with Ma at the house across from the park. I was sixteen or so, I guess. Belinda had a two or three year-old daughter named Karlie. Belinda's husband, Mack, had done a five-year stint in the joint for armed robbery. The fucking genius held up a grocery store on Christmas Eve, wearing his old army jacket. You know: the one with his name over the pocket? You might have noticed the discrepancy between jail time and childbirth. That seemed to be a big point of contention between them.

Because we were all partying, we all, well... partied.

I found myself in Mack and Belinda's apartment one night, along with Belinda and the neighbor's wife. The neighbor and

Mack were in Oregon. The store Mack had robbed and his stint in the joint had both been in Oregon. He had gone to retrieve some of his belongings up north.

The three of us started getting frisky. The neighbor gal was a bit too drunked-up, so she stumbled home while I was still at second base. Belinda changed into a nightie. I was rounding third when a pounding came upon the front door. She did a sneak peak around the far end of the curtain. She turned to me, her eyes as big as saucers and mouthed, "MACK!"

Well now, that's a fine fucking how d'ya do.

There was more pounding on the door.

I mouthed back to her, "I'm passed out," and flopped on the couch with my face in the cushions.

She opened the door and greeted him. I was blind to the room, but I didn't want to give myself away with an eye flicker.

"What the fuck is he doing here?" Mack asked with, shall we say, an *edge* to his voice.

Cool as a cucumber she says, "Shithead passed out. I couldn't wake him up.

"Fuck it, I went to bed."

He asked why it took her so long to answer the door and she again affirmed that she had been in bed.

Mack rousted me. I rolled over squinting, rubbing, "Wha, wha…?

"Oh fuck. What time is it?"

While I was speaking, I noticed the cartridge belts. There were two, slung bandito-style across his chest. Then there was the holstered gun. A Bowie knife rested in a scabbard on the other hip.

"Wow," I say, acting like I'm still trying to get my shit together. "You're loaded for bear."

"Damn, I think I'm still drunk!"

I don't know how I missed the long gun he had in his hand. He swung it up, across the coffee table in front of me. I looked down the barrel, wondering if I would see the bullet before it killed me. Mack was a pretty radical motherfucker.

He says, "What do you think of my new rifle?"

I looked above the barrel into Mack's eyes and smiled. I reached for the forestock, and he let go.

"Pretty cool, man. What caliber is it?"

I pulled the bolt back and the bullet that didn't have my name on it jumped out of the chamber.

"*Holy shit,* man! You could have blown my fucking *brains* out!

"Damn. You said it's four o'clock? Crap, I've got to be in auto shop in two hours. It was good to see ya, man. I'm glad you're back."

I kept babbling. Like my life depended on it.

"Damn, I'm still drunk. I gotta go, man... shit, I hope my car starts."

To this day, I believe that if I had panicked and blown it, he would have pulled the trigger.

They separated some time after that. It was shortly after that that I hit a home run with Belinda. That was back when I was living in the little trailer, a few feet away from Pop and Betty's bedroom window.

Yeah, that time. I figured I'd go look her up.

They told me she was shacked up with some guy. I knocked on the door of the address they gave me, anyway.

She answered.

He was at work. She had put on a pound or two, but it wasn't anything horrendous. There was a little red-headed girl wrapped around her leg. We sat at the kitchen table for about half an hour and chatted. I told her I was at Terry and Sis's for the next few days, then it would be back to Virginia. We said good-bye and parted.

It was that evening, while I was thinking about a girl named Patty, when Chaunce's phone rang.

It was Belinda. She wanted to know if I wanted to go out for a drink. In the backseat of a Toyota Celica, we did it more than we drank. Belinda was five feet eleven inches tall. I was six feet. The act was a feat.

I professed my love and asked if she would move to Virginia. I was thinking she might be a keeper.

Belinda moved out of dude's place and back in with her folks, and I went back to the boat.

The only real problem with her move to Virginia was that the ship was headed to the Mediterranean in a month or two. We would be gone for six months. What would be the point of renting an apartment given the situation?

We decide she'd come out for a five-day visit, and then we'd begin our half-year, long-distance relationship.

I rented a motel room for a few days, but didn't take any time off. I would need my leave for when I returned from the Mediterranean. The visit went well.

From the ship's store, I bought a pile of stationery and stamps.

Off to the Mediterranean

We went back out into the Atlantic for a bit more training before our deployment.

There was a fella from the Cats who used to get stoned with us over on the port side. Rags is what we called him. All that dude ever talked about was how the Navy sucked, and how he really wanted to go back home and marry his high school sweetheart. Every damned time I saw the guy, he'd begin the same old whine.

I got tired of it.

I figured I'd help him get the hell out. Now, the little story I'm about to tell is not a reflection on my opinion on gays in the service. I don't think I have one, actually.

It's simply the way it was. It's just what happened.

I told Rags to go to the Chaplain and tell him he was queer. He had to be sure to convince him of that *and* that he hadn't been aware of his sexual preference until *after* he had reported aboard.

That was important, in order to get around a fraudulent enlistment charge.

He then was to tell the sky pilot that he feared for his life. Some of his crewmates had discovered he was queer, and he was afraid they were going to throw him over the side. During my time of enlistment, gays on a ship were not tolerated. I don't care how many butt-fuckin' sailor jokes you've heard.

Honestly, when I laid out the plan to him, I was mostly being a smartass. I had lost patience with his constant bitching, moaning, and carrying on.

The next time I saw him, he told me he was being honorably discharged. I asked how the hell he had managed that and he looked surprised.

"What do you mean?," he asked. "It was your idea!"

Well, I'll be go to Hell...

There was another guy who was in the Gear for a short time who wanted out of the Navy. He wasn't in the Gear long. He had made some sort of complaint that we were being "mean" to him.

I dunno. I won't speak ill of the dead. I've no comment on the matter.

He not only transferred out of the Gear, but out of the division. He was moved to V-1, the handlers. Apparently, they were mean to him, too.

Again, no comment.

We were pulling in from the Atlantic when he jumped. We were in a channel, near the bridge and tunnel. There was a heavy fog. The water was extremely cold.

Witnesses said he sat down on the fantail, took his boots off and jumped.

Due to impaired visibility, it was improbable that a helo would find him, and they didn't.

He only had a half hour before hypothermia would have killed him anyway, if he didn't flat-out drown first. About a week later, they found him bobbing down by the piers.

It was a terrible waste of a life.

The Straits of Gibraltar are a trip. After a five-day Atlantic crossing, there's what looks like an inlet to a lake. Spain is to the north and Africa to the south. The opening into the Mediterranean Sea is only about eight miles wide. The first time through, I wondered why the hell we were taking a carrier into *there*. It doesn't take long before land once again is no longer in sight. We left Continental US (CONUS) September 29 and hit our first port, Rota, ten days later.

I also wondered why there was a shitload of hashish, but no pot. Blond Lebanese, the darker Italian, the African containing a swirl of white… no pot. Admiral Punk once paid five bones for a pinner joint. When he showed it to me, I almost mistook it for a toothpick. It was that skinny and dry. Must have been leftover contraband from the States. We tried to make it last as long as possible, savoring the flavor.

They called him Punk because he was about five-foot-nothing and he was a gawddamned Tasmanian Devil. Twice Punk caught me with his mumbling trick. Sometimes I *can* be a bit slow. The way it worked is he would walk up and say something. It would be garbled. Of course you'd be curious, and then he would motion you closer. To get closer, you had to bend over. By the time you were down there he already had the back of your topside jersey. This he would pull over your head and then slap the shit out o' ya. With great glee he'd run like hell.

Son of a bitch got me *twice.*

We were partying in One & Two one night. The shared One & Two space had become quite the party spot. There was an exhaust duct in the center of the space. In our complacency, we got to where we only stood at it when we were smoking weed, not hash. I'll tell you later about setting the ducting on fire.

Now that I think on it, I also split my head wide open on the damned thing. I'll get to that, too.

There was a desk at my end on the portside. The starboard and port doors—not hatches!—locked. At sea, after Ops, there wasn't much traffic aft on that level and frame. Also, where the port and starboard passageways passed by the three engine rooms (Four and the barricade, Number Three alone, One & Two), the passageways rose on a false deck above the cables. You could hear the hollow echo of footsteps if anyone walked through there.

So we got fairly stoned and decided to have our way with Punk. We hog-tied him and tossed him out in the port passageway, closing the door. He was tied up good. He struggled, but it was in vain. Now and again we'd hear steps coming. The struggling would stop and Punk would start pleading.

"Please untie me," he'd whine. "The rotten bastards… Please untie me."

Each and every time you'd hear a *thunk* as the person stepped over him and *clunk, clunk, clunk* as they proceeded on their way. I might have heard a snicker a time or two. Not one swinging dick would untie the guy.

Those guys were mean.

Yeah, and I caught that fucking duct on fire. It was weird shit, man.

No really. This was Stateside. We smoked a joint and instead of butting the roach, I let it go up into the suction. Even with the additional airflow, I figured the damned thing would beat itself out before it got wherever it was going to go. We went back down to the desk.

It might have been me who first noticed the smoke.

"Uh, guys…?"

Right after a bend, in the open end, the paint on the exterior was bubbling and smoking. The duct opening was at about eight feet above the deck. Someone climbed up on the CRO (Constant Runout Valve) chain drive guards and peeked in.

"I see yellow flickering."

Fuck-oh-dear.

Someone grabbed a fire extinguisher. I held him up while he discharged it into the duct.

We got lit up by static electricity.

It was a strange deal. Apparently the flow of CO_2 out of the horn, without the operator properly grounded, made some sort of static discharge. I mean *ZAP*, man! It almost knocked me down. At that point I figured *fuck it, call the fire party.*

I mean, I didn't want "burned down an aircraft carrier" on my resume. Ya know what I mean?

It was out by the time they got there. From a cursory inspection it was obvious there had been some real heat, though. They went ahead and pulled the grill from the opening and pulled out a burnt plastic toilet brush. No shit (sorry—couldn't help it). Now why the hell a toilet brush was in that duct in the first place—let alone why it was left behind there—is beyond me.

There was no sign of the roach and we didn't know shit.

"I walked in, saw smoke, and called it in," I said. "That's all I can tell ya."

There really isn't a whole hell of a lot to running an Arresting Gear engine. Like a damper, you do a lot of watching. Of course, with the engine, you also have weight settings to deal with. Every aircraft is set differently. The setting adjusts rate at which the CRO closes. The weight table is calibrated so that every aircraft stops within about the same runout distance, regardless of its weight (see below under hook running and wing catching—yes, wing catching).

The settings can be made in two ways. The primary method is by a paddle switch operating an electric motor. Up on the paddle the setting goes up. Down... The other is with a mechanical wheel. Never, ever, have the wheel in the engaged and locked position with your hand on it during a trap. It will spin like a fan as the crosshead moves and break your fingers—if they're still attached.

About the only setting I can recall these days is five-two-zero. That would be 52,000 lbs. for a Tomcat. Three-six-zero might have been an A-6. There's a setting for every type of bird. Four-two-five for an EA-6B? Hell, I dunno. I know I could do it with the toe of my boot, though. While sitting, of course. You didn't want to get caught, but it put on a good show for the Number One operator.

The way it works is that Primary calls down the setting on the phones. Remember the spots from the LSO platform?

"Set five-two-zero Tomcat."

The operators make the setting and then report back in order from Number One to Number Four. "One set five-two-zero." "Two set five-two…" Once all of the engines are set, that part of the program is done. If your engine takes the trap, "On Two with a one-seven-two." The one-seven-two would be the inches of ram travel. That and the aircraft type are logged while the engine is being retracted. When the engine is back to its original position the operator looks at a few indicators and then declares, "Battery."

"Battery" meant the machine was back in the ready position.

I slept through a trap while operating Number Two. It was when we were working that 95-hour day.

Ever work a 95-hour day? We were at ops for four days straight. The Gear didn't have enough personnel to run two shifts. The saving grace was that night ops were all anti-submarine. That's helicopters (helos) and S-3 Vikings. Vikings stayed in the air for several hours. Helos don't need no stinkin' Arresting Gear (though I've heard of an incident with a tail gear snag).

It was 18 hours in the machinery room, then a couple of hours on the barricade, a launch and arrestment, a couple of hours on the barricade, and then another 18 hours. Yeah, there was time to go to the mess decks. So, what's your point? Oh yeah! FOOD! Yeah, food. A little sleep would have been nice, too.

The barricades lay on a table in the space aft of the shop. Two tables, actually, one above the other. They measured about twelve feet across and twenty long. The top level was around chest height, and the lower just above the deck. Both surfaces were steel sheet, full of holes, very much like the deck on a catwalk, the flight deck's weather deck, so to speak.

There was a deck hatch at one end through which to pull one or the other barricade from the table to the flight deck—those handy tractors again. One barricade is for practice. The other is the real deal. The bottom shelf is dark. If a person wiggles around enough they can dig a form fitting nest in the nylon webbing. Believe it or not, folks had dibbies on their spots. Not just during this time, but any time. I heard Country fucked his girlfriend under there the day before we had left CONUS. A barricade drill would mean the nesting was back to square one. The spots were by grid location on the table.

The first day, of course, I hit the head for a quick shower and then went to my rack. Maybe the second too. That shit didn't work. Fuck the shower. Fuck you. I don't care. I'll be on the fuckin' barricade.

See, when sleep deprivation starts to catch up, all of the sudden an extra half hour of sleep is a hell of a lot more imperative than a bar of soap and a clean pair of drawers.

It got kinda bad. I'm not necessarily talking about my personal hygiene, but the attitude of the crewmen. Inadvertently bumping into someone in a passageway could start a fight. You could see the exhaustion in a person's eyes, and the caffeine.

Gator, "Drift, wake up man. You fell asleep."

Me, "Shit, piss, motherfucker. Unnh… what? *What?*"

Gator, "You took a trap, man. I called it. You're logged and set. You awake now?"

Me, "What'd you tell 'em?"

Gator, "Your phones are fucked up."

Good Ol' Gator.

Gator had been a car thief in Baltimore before joining the Navy. He had been happy being a car thief. It was when his, uh, organization decided to expand their business model to include armed robbery that Gator decided he wanted to go to work for a different, uh, company.

His employment wasn't the type of business where you tender your two week's notice. Gator enlisted in the Navy.

You might think that's really something, falling asleep in front of a trapping CRO valve, but Gator slept on a trapping engine—right on top of Number 2. We must have been running two shifts at the time. I was operating Two. I'm witness to the spectacle. I don't recall what his reasoning was. Gator got a little trippy sometimes; it probably doesn't really matter why.

He walked into the space and climbed up the engine, settled in between the cooler and accumulator, and laid down. Those are both side by side cylinders. They form a "valley" with about a four inch gap between the two.

"Yo, Gator, I'm catching planes here, man."

"Yeah, I'm quite aware of that, dumbshit. I'm going to lay up here and sleep. Do you mind?"

What was I going to say? "No?"

Not on your fucking life. I wanted to see this shit.

I watched him bounce up and down, trap after trap with the engine screaming, the crosshead banging and the cable, uh... cabling. He slept for hours. And when he got up he had a streak of grease and aluminum shavings four inches wide, down his back, from head to toe. He looked like the negative of a skunk.

We had two washing machines in the shop and a dryer in the barricade room (we called it a "room" not a "space"). You had to have pitched in on the cost of the machines—at least the last one purchased—in order to use them. Yeah, they weren't ship's equipment. They were machines like you'd buy at Sears. That came in real handy when your dungarees had other names, rather than your own, stenciled on them. Those were hard to get back from the ship's laundry.

Oh no, I didn't steal 'em. Remember my stolen blanket?

The dungarees I wore were mine, bought with my money from the Ship's store. I just didn't put my name on the damned things. I think I had one shirt with "Drift" stenciled on it. I did it on a whim. The fellas would try to talk me into crap like "Frankenstein" or some shit, but I normally went with Jones, Johnson, or Smith. Those were easy to remember. One wouldn't want to have to look down at their name to remember it.

I think the second washing machine was picked up when the first one started trashing our clothes. Arresting Gear machinery spaces and the flight deck are not clean working spaces. You and your clothes get hydraulic fluid (ethylene glycol), grease, jet fuel (kerosene) and anything else that wants to stick to it, on them. Putting a white tee shirt in the same machine work dungarees had been washed in was a risky proposition. So, we got a second machine for nothing but civvies.

The trashed machine became our work clothes machine. A five-gallon can of trichloroethylene sat beside it. We'd pour some of that, along with the detergent, into the machine. Trike's a good solvent for removing grease. That's why we got it in fivers. We also used it when our hands had the wire protectant on them.

Whatever that crap was, it's sticky. The solvent was the only thing that would take it off.

A word of warning about sitting on a fiver of trichlor: make sure the spout has never been opened and the can is totally sealed. In the machinery rooms, we'd use five-gallon cans for chairs quite often. I suppose it's because the molecule is small that trichloroethylene finds its way through things that would normally be considered tight, like an asshole. It'll waft up past the old sphincter and burn the hell out of your rectum.

It's terribly uncomfortable, and it's one of those deals where by the time you flash on what's going on, it's too late.

Most folks only do it once.

Before I recount the following I'd like to stipulate that in no way is it my intent to belittle Naval Aviators. They're some of the bravest people on the face of this earth. 'Kay?

When my little joke was over, it turned out I was the brunt of my own sense of humor. My fellow Arresting Gear crewmates would much rather have gone to the mess for a tray full of mystery meat than wait for the bolters and tanker.

A "bolter" is an aircraft that fails to engage the Arresting Gear. A "tanker" is an airborne fueling station. Bolt a couple of times and the gas gauge would be bouncing off of the "E."

It's not like you needed some sort of clearance to enter an Arresting Gear space. The machinery is rather simple and I'm sure not a secret to anyone. We just didn't care to have people in there who weren't Rats. Gear Rats, that was us. Rats are nasty little critters that peer at you from their dingy little holes. Our little holes just happened to house the equipment that would bring a Navy fighter to a stop on the proverbial dime and make change.

Or maybe it was because of the serious consequences should the equipment fail. A person doesn't let folks just wander around that type of machinery. For whatever reason, we were very protective of our machinery spaces. Almost to the point of neurosis, as you'll see.

The Arresting Gear engine rooms are aft, as you might guess. Three of them ran athwartships, on the O3 level (first below the flight deck), from the starboard to port passageway. Numbers One & Two were in the same space, which made things a bit crowded; Number Three had its own and Number Four was in with the barricade engine. The only engine room with two active engines was One and Two. I was operating Number Two.

Yeah, I told you that all-the-ready; I know. I'm just reminding.

The aft V-2 berthing space, called "the compartment" ran port/starboard as well. A curtain hung at each end, at the respective passageway. Port/starboard, starboard/port, athwartships, you know what I mean. Am I repeating myself?

There was a passageway quite a bit farther forward that ran port to starboard. I don't think I went up that way more than a few times. There was nothing for me that far forward. My whole world was aft. It was this forward passageway that pilots used to get to their ready rooms, from the starboard to port side.

So, from about amidships aft, the only way to get from one side of the boat to the other is the "passageway," then an engine room, V-2 berthing, and then two more engine rooms. Why all this talk about passageways? So I can tell ya the story! It's about passageways.

Sorta.

We were having a meeting in the shop when they told us the passageway up forward was closed. I don't recall why, but you couldn't cross there for the day. So I'm sitting there wondering what the hell that has to do with me, and why the Chief is looking at *me* while he's giving us what appears to be worthless information.

Then he says, "The pilots need to be able to get to their ready rooms."

Ah, oh. I have no idea what it is, but here it comes.

"Leave both doors open on 1&2. They'll be crossing there."

"Hang on here Chief, you want me to stay in the space and be a bell hop?"

"That shouldn't be an issue," says he. "They'll be crossing while we're operating."

I'll spare you the dialogue of the argument that followed. Suffice it to say I was an E-2 and he was The Chief.

Okay, fine. I have to do this, and do this I shall, I'm thinking. *Yep, you betcha. Heh.*

I know it wasn't the driver's fault, the Chief's fault or anybody's fault. It was what it was, but for some reason it pissed me off just a little. I mean, why couldn't they cross at Number Four or Number Three, or even the compartment?

Yeah, yeah, I was going to spare you all of that, wasn't I?

We used to get rags in big, wired bales. The bales were discarded civilian clothing that was hacked up. I knew an operator that had the back side of a pair of shorts hanging on the bulkhead in his engine room. Maybe you had to of been there to appreciate the true 'art' of the faded portion of those shorts? I'm getting side tracked. We went through a LOT of rags.

I started digging in the latest pile. When you cut the wires the bale becomes a pile. I found exactly what I was looking for; a big rectangle of cloth, purple in color.

Next I scrounged a top side helmet and stripped all the armor off of it, leaving only the skull cap liner. Then I grabbed a pair of goggles.

On the way down to my engine room I made a stop and borrowed the dark visor off a motorcycle helmet from one of my crew mates. I snapped the visor on to the previously bare liner.

Imagine you're a pilot. Imagine you've just stepped into a machinery room with two Arresting Gear engines. The space between the two engines can't be a full three feet and it's a fifty foot walk down the middle. You know these things jump and flat-ass *scream* when they take a trap. I'm here to tell ya, it'll scare the piss out of ya if you're not used to it. You also know your life is in the hands of the operators of these machines.

That's when you look to the port side as you pass the Number One operator on the starboard. The Number 2 operator, at the other end of the machinery room, is wearing a purple cape, tied at the throat, and he's bare-chested. Well, except for the Sun tattoo over his sternum.

He's wearing god-knows-what on his head. Snaps and flaps are flopping all over with exception to where the motocross visor is affixed just above the goggles he's wearing.

And he's cackling like a mad man as he makes the setting for the first aircraft. You hear him call into the phones, "Two set five-two-zero, Tomcat," then he looks at you and says, "Oh yeah, he's mine! All *mine!*"

And the operator starts cackling again. As you're trying to make the port passageway he screams, "HEADS UP!"

The deck jumps and you hear that banshee scream that seems to pierce your brain. Number 2 just took a trap (arrestment). The maniacal laughter fades off as you head down the passageway to your ready room for your mission brief. There were a bunch of pilots that came through there. Sometimes they passed in groups.

Now the way this works is, the drivers that just came through my space will be on the next launch. We called a launch and a recovery a "Go." These guys won't be the next we catch, but on the Go after.

Of course I don't need to tell you that The Chief caught wind of my antics and, uh—let's just say he wasn't pleased. After my ass chewing and the surrendering of my cape, it was business as usual. Hell, I'd even forgotten about it, mostly, when these guys started coming back aboard—the pilots who had crossed through earlier.

From Deck Edge, the DE operator is calling them in, "Long groove, short groove, over the ramp, *heads up!*" but then "Bolter, bolter, bolter."

Again and again and again. It seemed they were all flying down the deck, hitting beyond the Number Four wire. I thought it a bit odd, so many bolters, but it didn't dawn on me until the Number One operator, Gator, yelled at me.

"Drift, you son of a bitch!"

"What? What?"

"The last thing they want is Number 2. You son of a bitch!"

This is the guy who was yuckin' it up on the phones earlier.

"He's got a purple cape on! He's going fuckin' nuts!," he'd yelled. "It's too bad you guys are missing this."

Etc., etc. Yeah, the same guy.

Now, I'm a son of a bitch.

Pretty soon anyone with phones on is ragging on me.

"I'm pissin' in the drip pan, Drift. Ya know why I'm pissin' in the drip pan..?"

I really knew my ass was in the ringer when Pri-Fly called down.

"Two, Primary."

"Go Primary."

"They're launching the tanker, Drift. You *son* of a *bitch*."

That tanker just added another 1/2 hour or so to the Go. He'll be the last to trap after he's done fueling thirsty airplanes. What's another few minutes tacked on to what would have been an 18-hour day?

Some days things just don't work out the way you planned. Ya know what I mean?

One dark night one of the guys from the bow Cats stepped through a hole in a catwalk. A deck plate had been removed and not replaced. He fell sixty feet to the water. One of his buddies saw him go. Hell, he almost went with him. His body was never recovered. This was no scam. That young man was truly lost at sea. We hoped he had been knocked unconscious and drowned.

That would have been the most merciful death considering the circumstance.

We caught Vermin beating off. It was on the starboard side. Beyond One and Two dampers, moving forward, there's a small space, a void. You step through a hole cut through a frame, another not three feet later and you are in a space that opens out to the ship's exterior. The cables for number three elevator run through it. When the elevator's up you can see the water. When it's down the elevator and the water are visible. It's a good place to smoke hash or weed. In a like space over on the port side some bats set up house, once, when we were at the pier.

It was me, Cowboy, Stone and maybe Gator that had gone back there to blow a bowl. You know how it is when you get loaded? We got to bullshitting (now that I think about it, Gator had to've been there; that would explain the time spent BSing) and we were back there for some time. When we went to leave we checked to see if the next space was clear beyond that last frame.

There was Vermin. He had a fuck book in one hand and his dick in the other. There was a mop bucket between his legs. I thought that was awful decent of him. We watched, quietly giggling, for just a moment. There was a second there when I began to wonder if old Verm was beating off or trying to start a fire. Man, he was going to town.

We peeled back away from the frame penetration and consulted. We decided there was no good reason to bother the man when we could simply go blow another bowl. Assuredly, certainly, old Vermin would have reached his goal by the time we smoked a bit more. After all, we're all shipmates, right? You want'a help a buddy out, right?

We smoked. We even did some more bullshitting.

Vermin was still out there skinning his mule. Cowboy decided he had better things to do than wait until Verm popped a nut. He yelled at him.

"Vermin, you fuck! Turn the damned page or something, you dick-skinning son of a bitch!"

Verm's cock wilted like a plastic spoon in a microwave. The poor son of a bitch.

Loose lips sink ships? Loose lips almost got Vermin a write-up. We had gone to the shop and Cowboy was carrying on about the chicken choking he had just witnessed. I suppose we were all laughing about it.

1st Class Ruddy walked out of the office with some paperwork he wanted us to sign. He had been listening to us joking about Vermin's stroking and had actually written the man up for masturbating. The forms were witness statements. Can you believe that shit? He was going to write the guy up for loping his mule! We told him it was all fiction. It was a miscommunication about a joke we were going to pull. It never happened.

Write a man up for rubbing one out? That's the kind of shit that made me decide early on that I would be splitting when the contract was up. Unbelievable...

A lot of folks thought Ruddy was a prick. It's true he was an opinionated son of a bitch. It's also true that if you pissed him off he'd come gunning for you. I don't know why, and believe me I wasn't kissing his ass, but Ruddy and I always got along.

There was that time he found my pipe lying on a seat cushion in the shop. We had just popped back in (probably from getting stoned) and Ruddy announced he had found it. He proclaimed it had been a fine piece of work, then said he'd tossed it over the side.

He was looking at me the whole time. I've heard some claim that he never tossed it at all, but kept it. I suppose that was about the worst I got from him, other than being pestered about making rate.

He would carry on about responsibility... taking the test... yada, yada... My standard response was, "Man, you don't seem to understand," and I would hold my arms out looking around, "I'm just visiting."

We prided ourselves on our pipes and our knives.

The pipes we made from brass fittings and other crap appropriated from the tool crib. They weren't simple screw it together, put fire on one end, lips on the other affairs. We shaped them. We sculpted the fittings. The corners would be filed off the hex heads 'til they were round. We didn't stop at sandpaper; the final finish was done with Brasso.

You wanted yours small enough that you could easily cup it in your hand. Make it disappear, so to speak. It had to be able to hold at least half a gram of hash. You had to be able to light it without scorching any parts of the face. Major bonus points were awarded for meeting all of those criteria *and* being a nicely worked piece.

Mine—the one previously mentioned—had been voted the coolest. It was like a mini-Sherlock. There was the nicely fashioned brass bowl attached to the stainless steel stem onward to the brass bit and lip. I had wrapped copper wire around the stem in a fashion creating a spiral pattern from bowl to lip. It had the classic "S" shape.

It bummed me when I lost it. I can't bitch too much about Ruddy. Shit happens. There was a lot of posturing to determine which the next winning pipe would be. I think the fellas decided no one was worthy of the crown. The king is dead, and that's that.

We carved our buck knives, too; shaping the handles to fit our fingers. We would sharpen the blades with stones, then take the grit and introduce it to the blade handle hinge point and work it. The goal was to make it so the blade could be easily flicked open. Hey, we were kids, okay?

Unfortunately, that screwed up the blade locking mechanism, too. Unfortunate—unless you got caught at a concert smoking weed.

It was me and one of the other Three Musketeers—Fred, Gator or Stone—attending a concert at the Scope in Norfolk, Virginia. We had aisle seats. I had just passed the joint to my companion when I felt a tapping upon the top of my head. I looked over to the steps and saw a pair of grey slacks, with a black stripe running down them. I thought maybe if I just didn't look up, didn't make eye contact... My companion passed the number down the row.

Whew.

And then, *tap, tap, tap.*

Fuck.

Eye contact it is. The copper points at the two of us and gives us the come hither finger. He followed us out of the arena and herded us to a spot. He does all of the name asking and whose command are you under and all of that shit. Then he starts threatening us with calling our Captain. Then he spied my Buck knife on my belt. He asked that I hand it to him. I did. The cat starts to tell me he's going to take me to jail (we didn't have any weed on us. It was my last joint) because a lock blade knife was illegal. I said it wasn't. He started to do his thing about how *he* should know the law.

"No, man," I says. "I'm telling you it's not a lock blade."

"Bullshit," he says. "These are lock blade knives." He opened it. "You have to push here to close the blade."

"Lay the back of the blade on your palm and gently push. Make sure your fingers are out of the way." The blade folded like a snitch under hot lights. He was fairly pissed off but he gave the knife back and let us go.

The copper had nuthin' on us.

THE DECK

The Topside Crew was a bit of a prima donna outfit. Colorado Ron, the Topside PO made damn sure of it. Petty Officer 2nd Class Ron had transferred over from the Army. It was said that while there he was decorated while in combat. Someone was pitching a beef about him one day when I overheard a Chief exclaim, "Are you kidding? The man's a motherfucking hero!"

Hero or not he was a touch, uh, eccentric.

He kept a grease gun, loaded with high temp grease, lying beside the coffee pot. Whenever he made a pot he always put a shot on top of the grounds.

"Grease is the lifeblood of the Gear," he'd yell. "By God you'll have it running through your veins!"

I'm not bullshitting you. I have witnesses. People would routinely ask who made the sludge before getting a cup; people that knew, anyway. We tried stashing the gun once. That doesn't work while within a few steps of machinery whose lifeblood is high temp grease. 'Sides, the fucker would throw a fit.

Everyone besides the topside guys—except maybe the maintenance crew of three to five guys—had a machinery space they could call their own, though the "M" Crew had the run of the joint while we were rackin' and they were wrenchin'.

PO2 Ron decided the shop belonged to the topside crew. He decided it was the topside club house. Whomever was working in Primary was considered somewhat part of topside—the red headed stepchild. No others needed apply.

There was a TV in the shop. During ops, it would be turned to the deck cameras. After ops, there was other closed circuit programming. Late at night sometimes an "R-ish" flick would get snuck in. Obviously, the coffee pot was in the shop.

Another cool thing about the shop was that it was only a few short steps down the passageway to the flight deck catwalk. "So what?," you might be thinking.

Well, the closest head was clear over on the port side. Everyone pissed off of (or in) the catwalk. There was a corner over behind the fire hose stowage. Two of the things you had to be careful of on the weather deck were the wind and the seas. If the wind was just right a person might whip it out, let loose and find themselves with a face covered in piss. I've had sea water come up through the catwalk and drench my legs. Yeah, water clear up the hull to there. Cool, huh? The flight deck catwalk is a weather deck made of holed plate. You can stand and look straight down at the ocean between your feet.

Out of boredom there were times in port that I would stand in the same catwalk, with a handful of fasteners from the tool crib, and bomb jellyfish. It takes eight direct hits with 3/4 inch nuts to sink one of about two feet in diameter. Bolts are better. They create more damage as they rip through.

I'd hold my arm steady on the handrail, aiming through a sight created by my thumb and forefinger. -Bombs away! Direct hit!-

Yeah, I know it sounds terribly cruel. No, I've never tortured kittens, pulled the wings from a fly or fried ants with a magnifying glass. I got stung by a jelly once. I was extracting vengeance.

I had to quit. The maintenance crew was beginning to ask questions about the missing fasteners.

I'm getting sidetracked, on a tangent... I digress! Lets' get back to Colorado Ron's Club House, shall we?

It's true there was a TV in the berthing compartment but there was also only a table and about four chairs. The no-loads (fuck ups) had to have a spot, right? And what if a group of guys wanted to play cards?

I think it was when Ron kicked another PO out of "his" shop that the exclusive club took a thumping. The cat had come in to grab a cup of coffee and stood for a bit watching the TV program. Ron was in an exceptionally foul mood.

"You've got your fucking coffee, now get the hell out."

"What?" Dude was confused. "Pardon me?"

"This space belongs to the topside crew. Get. The. Hell. Out."

It wasn't but a day or two after that little confrontation that you had to get into the shop early for the movies or you wouldn't get a seat. Colorado Ron had gone a bit far and lost. The club house became open admittance.

I started on deck as his Safety. That's the way he liked to do it so that he could evaluate you person to person. I find no fault in that a'tall. That's the way I'd do it. A new man on deck is a bit of a liability until you know where he's at. If Ron didn't think you cut the mustard, then it was back into the steel cave. Down the rat holes you went.

It's a bit tough for me to explain the intuition of working on the flight deck of an aircraft carrier. You can't hear shit, yet you listen to everything. You learn how to tell what direction an aircraft moving behind you is headed and how far away it is, all while you can't hear the man standing in front of you yelling.

There's a rhythm. Even without looking forward, you know when the last plane has launched off of the bow. After the last waist launch, you know how long it'll be before the first trap makes its approach. If there's a glitch anywhere along the way you look to see why, what. Sudden movement out of the corner of your eye…

You move amongst taxiing aircraft. You know from the rhythm where the plane you are trying to get past is going to be headed. You know whether to stop or go, and where.

You never put your hands in your pockets. You never walk along looking down. You have your head up and you are looking at *everything* at *once*. You are hypersensitive, but at the same time you are filtering the information.

It's a fuckin' trip, man.

One of my favorite gags (though short lived) was to be walking along, hands in the pockets and looking at my feet. You'd be surprised how many people would notice. It was the behavior of an idiot or someone new to the deck, or both. A time or two, out of the corner of my eye, I even caught someone pointing me out to another crew member. Then they would begin to freak when they realized I was walking right into the exhaust of an aircraft. Like, real close to where it leaves the plane.

That could very well create havoc. A man blown down from that close is most likely going to receive some sort of injury, whether burns, ripped skin from the non-skid on the deck, or even possibly a broken bone from being tossed. Another aspect was where was the individual going to be blown to? Under the wheels of another moving aircraft, into an intake? Depending upon the location on the deck, maybe over the side.

Though still looking down, I'd be catching the action around me. Folks would already be moving to do something. They might not know what, but they figured as soon as I took three more steps *something* would need to be done.

Right as I reached that point, I would tuck my shoulder and roll under the rear of the aircraft, pop up (unscathed) on the other side and continue my stroll; hands still in the pockets, still watching my toes, possibly whistling.

They caught on pretty quick. It only worked a few times. I only moved about in Fly II and III. I suppose I could have gone up to the bow Cats (Fly I), and run the gag a time or two, but that was too damned far to walk.

And then there was the physical aspect of working the deck in Arresting Gear.

A CDP weighs about 3-1/2 pounds per foot without considering the terminal end. Should a CDP (it's the Cross Deck Pendant, remember?) need to be stripped, it'll almost always be the topside PO and the Safety that initiate it.

The Hook Runner comes down the Foul Line to help. Maybe a Deck Edge operator will be able to assist. The whole time the wire is being broken loose and pulled off, everyone is counting the planes that are being waved off. The wire is typically only broken loose from the purchase cable/CDP connection on the port side, then dragged to starboard. That puts the CDP clear of the landing area.

During a recovery, if the CDP is to be changed rather than just stripped, things get a bit tougher. It can be a real bitch when one is stripped and replaced during a Go. It wasn't uncommon to pull one and then replace it a few traps later during a gap in the pattern. Providing, that is, it was yanked due to a damaged wire and not a downed engine. Engine downs do happen, but a trashed wire is far more likely. For the Hook Runner, that would mean two trips down the Foul Line and back, *and* that whole hook running thing.

Around 400 lbs for four guys doesn't sound like much, but remember at least two of them had to run a few hundred feet to get there. And as soon as the wire is stripped, the deck will go clear and it would be nice if you were back where you where supposed to be at that time. Hook running is, by far, the most physical Arresting Gear topside watch station. I'll get there after a while.

There's always a standby tractor waiting by the barricade hatch. It's there to pull the barricade from the table or to pull a wire so there's enough slack to decouple and to drag a new CDP across the deck. The tractor will only get the new CDP close. The tractor doesn't pull the disconnected CDP from the deck. It's faster for everyone to grab the thing and drag it off.

As the new guy, you got the shit jobs. The CDPs come in a box. A spare CDP has to be ready at all times. That could mean being stuck wiping the protective coating off of the new CDP fitting while everyone else was headed below. Topside sheave greasing was normally a rotational thing. It took me a while to learn that it was customary to stick the new guy with everything you possibly could until he wised up.

Once you had Colorado Ron's nod, then it was up to the rest of the crew to decide if they would have you. I was in. From Safety I went to the LSO platform. Fee-Fee checked me out.

I think Fee-Fee was from Brooklyn or New York or some fuckin' place where they have an accent. Hell, maybe he just had a speech impediment, I don't know. They called him Fee-Fee because of a haircut he had gotten once.

Fee-Fee had the kinky hair like a black man's. He got a Marine-style "high and tight" once and it made him look like a damned poodle. He got stuck with "Fee-Fee."

He really wasn't a very good teacher.

You got checked out on watch stations during ops. It's tough to dry run plane catching. The two of us got over to the platform a bit early, and screwed in our phones. He told me about spotting; where on the portside to start calling them from and how; how to tell a stretch from an A-6, an F-8 from a Corsair. He then explained that after Punk (Primary) told me that the Gear and Lens were set, I was to call out to the LSOs, "Gearlenziazet, gear down, hook down, clear deck."

I figured " gearlenziazet" was like some sort of short hand. Hell, I didn't know, but if Fee says that's what I'm to say, hey?

He did the first couple of planes as he had described and then it was my turn.

I did a couple and then an LSO turned around and asked, "What the fuck did you say?"

I shrugged, "hook down, gear down?"

"No. That other shit."

"Gearlenziazet?"

"Yeah, what the hell is "Gearlenziazet?"

Fee-Fee jumps in, "It's his accent sir. He's saying, Gear. Lens. Set."

Shit-oh-dear. Something about that whole thing just wasn't right. And what the hell was a lens?

I didn't stand the LSO watch for long. It wasn't that I blew it or anything. It just wasn't my cup of tea and if I remember correctly someone on Deck Edge wanted to move across the deck. It might have been Lil' Ski.

That place was sort of a pilot yuppie hangout spot or something. There were always more pilots than were required. I thought it dangerous from time to time, or should I say the full platform increased that factor?

Before I went to work on deck, I remember Country doing three days on bread and water because he walked off of the platform. He had bitched and bitched about the crowding. Finally he threatened and made good with it. He just walked the fuck off. It created quite the stir. There was a crowd in the shop to greet Country with applause when he returned from the brig.

Deck Edge isn't as gravy a watch station as the platform, but it is a stationary position. There are retract handles to pull, but that doesn't take a whole hell of a lot. In bad weather sometimes you'd luck out and the tail section of an aircraft would be spotted over you for cover. Deck Edge and Primary are the only two in contact with the machinery rooms. LSO talked to Primary only. The Topside PO has communication with the Boss and the Gear Officer over a radio, but no phones. The Safety and Hook Runner have no audio communication at all.

Deck Edge would bitch to the machinery rooms about the rain, or snow, or freezing-assed wind or what have you. You would invariably hear back, "Twenty-five dollars a month." That was the extra pay for hazardous duty.

That reminds me about that fucking Obie. The guy's first name was Roger. The first couple of times that I heard him come back on the phones with "what?," I thought it was funny. He did it for over a year before he was forced to quit doing it. Obie had begun to get threats of violence.

We'd get stoned under Deck Edge before a Go.

A "Go?" That would be one cycle, a launch and a recovery. With every launch there's a recovery immediately following (the planes launched on the previous go), with exception to the first launch and the last recovery. With the first launch there isn't anything to recover. They've just left on their mission. With the last recovery—if there had been a launch then it wouldn't have been the last recovery, now would it? You get it. Didn't I explain "go" back at the engine room? Well, just in case you missed it…

I know I didn't mention that the Arresting Gear watch stations were always manned during any launch. Just because the damned plane had been flung into the air didn't necessarily mean it was going to want to fly. If he could make it back around V-1 would have cleared the Waist and we would be ready to recover him.

Wasn't I talking about getting stoned before a Go? Yeah… yeah, I was.

Remember I told you about the weather deck the emergency chute went to? You could climb back up hand over hand on the pole. It *was* a bitch though. I liked to pinch the corner off of a gram of hash, swallow the rest and then smoke the pinch. We were down there and it looked like everyone had their own pipe going so that's what I went to do. I took off a pinch and tossed the rest down the gullet. It hung up and I did one of those involuntary puke things; right at everyone's feet. That was kind of gross. It wasn't until I spied the hash sitting there, in the midst of my lunch, picked it up and tossed it back down that Cowboy puked.

⚓ ⚓ ⚓

Tripping directors from Deck Edge was great fun. Well, new directors or dumb ones, I guess. They way it worked was that Deck Edge set up while planes were still launching. Directors would be taxiing aircraft aft still. You'd watch the director as he walked backwards toward a wire. He would glance back to see where it was. That's when you reached over and raised the wire supports. In his mind, the wire is lying on the deck. You just put it at about an eight to ten inch elevation. Director snags a heel and goes down. The guys on Deck Edge busted a gut laughing and pointed at the pissed off director.

Hey, we were young, okay?

More great fun was knocking people down with a wire retract after a function. We'd try to warn them. We'd yell and wave then give the retract signal. If at that point a person stepped into it, well, bummer deal. Down they would go, to much laughter.

Burnie took over Topside PO after I had gone to Deck Edge, I think. Something like that. I had been broken in as the Safety, checked out on LSO and now was a fully fledged Deck Edge operator. I was working on the deck.

Burnie became my boss.

Burn was from a small Indiana town. He had been the drum Major in the high school he'd graduated from at 17 years of age. There was no money available for further education. His dad told him he could get him on at the steel mill. Burn didn't want to do that. Burnie went to see the Navy recruiter.

I was an Arresting Gear deck hand! Topside Crew! But the job I wanted was a little further up the Foul Line. Typically, the Hook Runner was a watch station. Not necessarily one person. Commonly, the station was switched off between three people or so. Someone would run hooks for a few Goes, then someone else would do it for a while. It was a rotation, like greasing topside sheaves. No one *wanted* to do it.

It's the Hook Runner who gets killed or maimed when shit goes wrong. Like I said, it can be a physically challenging station, too. I think I had gotten checked out on hooks after Burn took over, but then I'm pretty sure it was a fella from the old guard who checked me out.

I suppose it doesn't matter. I took right to it.

THE HOOK RUNNER

I told Burn I was the new Hook Runner. He didn't understand me at first.

"Leave me on the Foul Line, man. Period. No Deck Edge. No platform or Safety. I'll run hooks all o' the time." I was serious, but he didn't believe me. "I wanna be The Hook Runner."

"Are you fucking nuts?"

"That has no bearing on this conversation."

"You're fucking nuts. You're not right in the head a'tall. I don't give a shit, you wanna run hooks, run hooks. You can switch off any time. Just say the word."

You are alone when running hooks. You stand 100 feet forward of Crash & Smash (the emergency crew) and 50 or so feet aft of the Gear Puller. One man, all alone standing in the open as an aircraft comes screaming toward him half out of control. I still think it's the coolest fucking job in the world.

Maybe I am nuts.

I didn't know at the time that they were just trying to screw with my head when they told me some crap about a legendary Hook Runner who caught wings. It seems this nameless individual would grab the leading edge of the wings as they leaned in on the wire. "Leaning on the wire" is when, at the end of the runout, the Gear engine has stopped but the aircraft hasn't... quite. The wire stretches. If you pay attention you can watch the cable as it twists and thins: "leaning on the wire."

It took me a couple of days to perfect it.

The Three Wire is the target wire. I started paying close attention to where different aircraft stopped when they trapped Three. Remember that thing about the CRO valve being designed to stop planes in about the same spot? They really do, pretty much, do that. I took notice of my position on the Foul Line. I practiced in my head as planes trapped.

I could have caught that one. If I had been standing in front of the wing I would have *caught it.*

I started at the wing tips and slowly moved farther inward. I found that I had to actually sprint from the Foul Line to get there in time. Charging out early made it easier. I'd get my ass chewed fairly regularly for being out in the landing area a bit too early.

It's embarrassing as hell to be standing out on the deck with your hand up and watch the hook skip Number Three and Four.

It ain't gonna stop, man.

On my end it wasn't a big deal. All I had to do was kneel down and the wing would pass over my head at about 150 mph, the aircraft going back airborne at the end of the angle deck. I suppose it looked pretty dramatic from the tower though.

I turned running hooks into a visual performance art. A fucking ballet. The dancing company consisted of F-14s, A-7s, A-6s, EA6Bs... any wing above my head that I could grab. To step in front of an F-8 Crusader would have been Russian Roulette. The wing's height comes within a man's body. I'm not *that* nuts.

Imagine, if you will, an aircraft slamming onto the deck. They're supposed to do that. How else to plant yourself when the "ground" is moving away beneath you? Yep, when the deck's coming the other way it can be a bit more of a slam. It's all part of the dance.

The hook and the main gear normally make contact about the same time. Upon engagement, the hook begins to move upward toward the fuselage as the main gear absorbs the impact. The hook sends a spray of sparks and nonskid behind the plane. The tires of the main gear let off puffs of smoke as they try to catch up with the aircraft's forward motion.

Though he's still moving at 150 mph, he firewalls it to full Military Power (no afterburner). If the hook doesn't engage the wire, he'd better have the juice to get back air borne.

The nose most likely will have settled or be setting down when the hook engages the wire.

The nose gear of the plane compresses heavily as the aircraft realizes the trap.

The path of the wire deforms. As it's pulled the CDP/Purchase cable connections are sucked toward the center line of the deck. It looks more the steep bell curve than a triangle. Does that make sense? In a split second they'll be thrown back outward. Maybe a whip effect would be a better description?

There's smoke, there's wire being played out, there's an aircraft on the end of it all that will be coming to an abrupt stop, uh, when everything quits moving. Standing in the angle deck, mid-wing of the bird, is some crazy bastard with his hand in the air. The screaming aircraft, knowing it's caught, gives up the fight as the crazy bastard grabs a hand full of the leading edge of the wing. As the stretch in the wire relaxes he gives the wing a push as the wire itself pulls the plane back a few feet. The effect being that the crazy bastard made the final stop and then, half in disgust, shoved the plane away.

"Is that all you've got?"

A ballet, man. A dance that requires you be on your toes... That's ballet? Right?

Number Four traps weren't an issue. The plane *was* slowing. It *was* going to stop, it would just be behind me. I'd let my hand slide along the bottom of the wing as it passed. No problem.

Oh crap. You don't know who or what running hooks is! Silly me.

During arrestments the aircraft "belongs" to the gear until such time that it's handed off to a director, called the Gear Puller. The plane traps and runs out. There's a fella whose job it is to ensure it's cleanly released from the wire and handed off to the puller who in turn gets it out of the landing area as soon as possible.

On a typical trap, the Hook Runner approaches with his open hand (the catching hand) in the air above his head and shoulder. This signal means, "I have command." He then watches the aircraft and wire, at the right moment he makes a sweeping motion with his arm.

The Hook Runner holds his thumb out like a hitchhiker. This is the signal for "hook up." Hopefully, the hook and wire separate with no drama. The Runner then passes the aircraft to the Puller. This is done simply by pointing at him.

"The plane's yours, man."

Once the plane is clear, the Hook Runner swings his arm round and round. He's signaling Deck Edge, way down yonder, to retract the engine. The aircraft is now on the move, out of the area. With the wire on its way back, job done.

Most of the time.

If the ship rolled to port just right, while the cable was on deck, the damned purchase cable would fall into the Number Three Cat track. That would prompt a "foul deck" signal (arms crossed overhead, stopping the retract) and the cable would have to be removed—quickly!—before the retract could resume.

How many pounds per foot did I say a CDP weighed? The purchase cable has to be close to the same. Pulling 75 feet of it out of a narrow trough is a *bitch*. Yeah, with planes being waved off and passing overhead. How many now? Two? Landing pilots can be impatient. I've felt the blast down the neck of my flight deck jersey as they went over.

After the retract, I had a John Wayne walk I used as I ambled back to the Foul Line. I'd have to be back across before the plane was out of the landing area and the wire was at battery. That still left plenty of time for the swagger.

I was a showman. I was the shit. No one had ever done it the way I did. When a plane trapped, all eyes were on that aircraft because the show was at the end of the runout. With their bullshit stories, the fellas had created a freak.

Seriously. No shit. I'm not telling you something that's not true. You can ask any of the fellas. If you send me a self addressed stamped envelope, with five dollars, I'll send you the email address to fifteen of 'em. Sorry guys—I'm just trying to make a buck here.

The PLATT and Lens guys got pissy whenever they had to go on deck and wipe off the glass window for their deck cameras. They used the excuse that they didn't get hazardous duty pay, so the task of cleaning their window should fall to somebody else.

You've seen video from an aircraft carrier deck camera, I'm sure. You might not realize that those cross hairs change for each type of aircraft. That's what PLATT and Lens does. They don't do windows. Some bright bastard mentioned that I always walked up the center line after checking the four wire, anyway. I could just go ahead and wipe the camera windows while I was there.

Before a Go, the cat working the platform would walk the Number One wire. He would check that the connection to the purchase cable was as it should be. He would inspect to see that any broken strands in the CDP were within tolerances, blah, blah.

The Safety would normally do Two. The Topside PO would check Three, and the Hook Runner would look in on Number Four, the furthest wire forward.

Walking up the angle deck was one of my favorite times.

There would be good wind over the deck. I could release the snaps on my float coat, hold it open with my arms and lean into the wind. I could achieve ridiculous forward lean angles standing there. It would be quiet. The launch would be over. The aircraft to recover wouldn't even be in view yet.

There was the sea.

I must admit, I miss the sea. The "sea" is some sort of all-encompassing word for those who understand. I so enjoyed the sea. A dichotomy existed. Standing on one of the largest killing machines known to man, I existed in complete peace. I dig that kind of shit.

I realized that, while I was wiping the glass, I was being broadcast on ship CCTV. Heh. For the window cleaning, I did Charlie Chaplin. A little dance up to the camera. A big show of shaking out the rag I pulled from my pocket. A production of dragging up the spit to dampen the rag (I never actually spit on the rag but once; all it did was make a mess). A thumbs up to the camera, indicating the window was clear. Job well done!

Of course I'd mix it up. I didn't want to be too predictable to the thronging crowds.

Burnie had tubes of paint. I don't know what kind of paint. Something a person would apply to a canvas, I suppose. Paint for paintings. I painted on the back of my float coat. The representation was that of King Kong on the Empire State Building swatting planes. I'm sure you get the connotation. I painted Fred and Cowboy's coats, too.

Fred had become the Fly Two Tractor King. His responsibility was coordinating the movements of the Yellow Gear (i.e. tractors) within his area. On the back of his flotation device, I painted a tractor with big-assed slicks on it and a blower poking up out of the hood. Fred Flintstone was looking around the blower.

Cowboy's coat got a goofy looking bird, wearing a flier cap and goggles, looking at you while flying into the fantail. The caption underneath read, "Huh?" It might not sound like a good fit, unless you'd seen Cowboy get really fuckin' loaded.

With those same paints, I replaced the hooker who was rendered on the shop door. Our new Captain didn't think such things were appropriate. My offering was a parchment with Mother Teresa's classic, "We the willing, led by the unknowing…"

Later, on the aft bulkhead of the shop, Burnie and I painted a mural. It measured about five feet tall by ten long.

The sun was setting on the sea, its red and yellow rays running across the waves toward you. Just right of center, in the foreground, was an old biplane making a turn. There were other aircraft about, at further distances. In the background, to the left of the sun, steamed an old flattop carrier. It looked pretty damned cool, if I may say so myself.

Burnie was part of the *America*'s decommissioning prior to her intentional sinking in '05. He said it had been painted over grey, but if you knew, you could see the texture of our paint under the grey.

Saying that you fucked up because you were loaded was never an excuse. If a person couldn't do his job because he was stoned, then he shouldn't have been stoned: plain and simple. Folks who couldn't do their job stoned *or* straight became compartment cleaners and what-not.

Someone has to clean the decks and scrub the head. Those guys were known as "No-Loads." A No-Load is when they fire the catapult, uh… without a load. It's kind of like functioning an Arresting Gear engine. These cats didn't pull their weight.

I'm getting off track here, though.

There were at least two incidents where I saw a "bye" given. Not so much that the fucked up individual(s) had fucked-up, but that they were just too fucked up. I'll tell you about one such event here. For the other, you'll have to wait a chapter or few.

We were functioning an engine after a rereeve. The purchase cable had been replaced (rereeved), and we were giving it a yank to make sure someone hadn't left a wrench in the works. On deck were me, Burnie and C.O. I don't recall who was on Deck Edge.

Burn and C.O. had done a hit of mescaline. I didn't get any. I'm still pissed about that. I mean, you'd have thought they both could have broken me a little piece off, or something.

Burn was back by the sheave. C.O. was driving the tractor that was pulling the wire, and I was up about where I thought the tractor would start spinning out and that would be that. C.O. had grabbed a Crash & Smash tractor rather than a tow rig. The crash tractor was extended in the rear for firefighting equipment. It was heavier than a tow, and most of that extra weight was behind the rear wheels. With that extra traction, they could pull more wire. He pulled all he was going to get. He backed up enough so that I could yank our hook from the pintle and wire and chuck it onto the tractor.

It was when Chunky (the "C" in C.O. stands for Chunky. The "O," his last name) was free of the wire and went to spin around that I saw the fire. Something under the chassis was burning. A red flame licked up the side of the rig. I yelled at Chunky.

"C.O.! You're on fire, man!"

C.O. stopped, got off the tractor and checked himself, then sat back in the seat.

"No I'm not."

Ah, crap.

"Not you, dammit, the fucking tractor. The *tractor's* on fire!"

Another lick of flame swept up the side of the tractor, this time on the operator's side. Chunky now understood, but he was also lost. It was like he was in a panic. I knew what he really was; he was higher than a kite. I yelled at him again.

"Bring it over here! Come here!"

He had been 50 feet or so from me and driving aimlessly. I wasn't going to try to chase him down. C.O. did as I asked. He drove right over. He then jumped out of the seat and ran like hell. This would have been fine and dandy, 'cept for one little detail.

The right front tire of the rig had my steel-toed boot trapped. He had parked on my foot.

By now, Burnie had come forward on the deck to see what all of the fuss is about. He and Chunky stood together, about thirty feet away. I overheard C.O. tell him the thing was burning , but I was going to put it out.

They both seemed rather comfortable with that plan.

I yanked my foot almost hard enough to pull a joint out of socket. No joy. I tried to twist it. Still no joy. I was trapped. I reached as far as I possibly could and came up about a foot short of the onboard fire extinguisher. I was stuck to a goddamned burning piece of firefighting equipment.

Shit-oh-dear.

I yelled over to C.O., "You parked on my foot!

"I'm stuck. I need you to come and move it off of my foot."

I was trying to stay calm. I could tell the bastards were peaking, just by looking at them. I needed to get through the haze. Find the light switch and turn it on.

C.O. yells back, "I'm not going over there, Drift. That tractor's on fire!"

Crap.

"I know, that's why I need you to move it. I'm stuck here. I can't do anything."

Burnie pipes up with, "Hey Drift, aren't you going to put out that fire?"

"GODDAMNIT! IT'S ON MY FUCKING FOOT!"

They stood there. They were spectators and by gum that's exactly all they intended to be. They were villagers watching the Drift burned at the tractor. Er... somethin' like that.

I was wondering how long it would take me to cut my foot off with my pocket knife and whether I'd bleed to death before I could get a tourniquet on it. And then there was that whole, "that's going to hurt like a sumbitch" and "I'd like to keep that foot" thing, too. It was while I was making these considerations that I noticed the fire had gone out. Whatever had torched off was spent.

Burnie walked over to the tractor, took a blank look at me and said, "Fire's out."

He jumped into the driver's seat and drove off.

IT'S NOT JUST A JOB...

The launch off the waist was about done. I was thinking about walking the Four Wire for an inspection when I heard, *"BOOM!"*

It caught my immediate attention. Loud booms on the deck have a tendency to do that—catch a person's attention. Flaming chunks of, uh, something were being flung over the Number Four Jet Blast Deflector. A Tommy getting ready to launch had FOD'ed. The acronym is for Foreign Object Damage. Something solid had been sucked into the intake.

This was one of those instances when one might be trying to decide whether to flat out run like hell, or to get to a firefighting station and grab a hose. I mean, when something spinning at, like, a bazillion RPMs starts coming apart... and there's fuel... and there's unexpended ordnance...

The pilot (or the plane) shut it down. It was over almost as soon as it had started. A couple of the LSOs who had begun to gather over on the platform were stomping out the flames of whatever had come over the JBD.

Turned out it was plastic. Topside hats—cranial helmets—are made of plastic and fabric.

It was chunks of the Hookup & Holdback's topside hat. He'd had his head up his ass for just one second, and then found it to be in the intake of a wound-up F-14. That's all it took up there. One little "oops."

"Oops" could be a *real* bitch.

There was a different exit path from under each type of aircraft as it prepared for the Cat shot. The planes were spun up at full power. When the deck was wet, you could see little vortices of water being sucked into the maw. Even with ear protection, a person could hear the air screaming as it was pulled down the intake. It's some serious shit, man.

The Holdback would come out from under, and then the Safety last. This time, the Holdback came out in the wrong spot: dead in front of the port intake. His feet left the ground and his head went straight up the intake. The Safety did the "save him from being run over by a bus" tackle.

Sorta.

He dove and grabbed the Holdback by the legs, dragging him out of the dragon's mouth. The helmet was ripped from the hold-back's head. BOOM!

Hello, Holdback! Good bye, jet engine.

It was no big deal, really. I guess. The squadrons always bring a spare engine or two.

The retract valves on the arresting gear engines always seemed to be a problem. The damned things never sealed all the way, so an engine would always walk back. That is, without anyone telling it to, the engine would slowly work itself back to battery.

That could be a problem when you wanted to change out a CDP. It was tough to make the hook-up when the purchase cable was running away from ya. In the extreme, it could be an issue when a plane trapped. If the engine started to walk back before the plane came off of the "lean," the tension would never release enough for the wire to drop from the hook. The issue could be mitigated during a CDP change by the engine operator closing the isolation valves to the retract valve. Typically, a member of the crew doing the change would signal Deck Edge to tell the operator to close his "globe" valves. At the appropriate time, the deck hand would signal for the valves to be opened. A few moments later, the full retract signal would be given. That was SOP.

When the walkback got terribly bad, the M (maintenance) Crew would get a "work order."

We had a "Stretch" (an EA6B) with a bad hook dampener. That meant its hook was just kind of swinging in the breeze. There were no forces pushing it downward, holding it in place. It was a limp dick. The limp dick had taken out Number Four. It had partially engaged and then spit the wire, trashing out the CDP. Four had been stripped. Limp Dick then made another pass and took out Number Three.

Having One and Two only was not optimal. There's that whole "flirting with the fantail" thing and stuff. The Boss wanted Three back on mighty quick. Three had walked back to where the barrels were against the topside sheaves. In other words, the distance between the two ends of the purchase cables was longer than the CDP. That took some fucking around with a tractor.

That took too much time when we were in the middle of a recovery, so it was decided that Four would go back. Burnie gave me the heads up, "After the next plane, we're putting Four back on," with his hands. I was up the Foul Line, after all.

The tractor pulled the CDP across the deck.

First wave-off.

Burnie went to the port side alone while the Safety and me tackled hooking up the starboard.

Another plane waved off.

We were done. We were good. We looked over at Burn, and he told us to signal for the valve opening. He still had the CDP/purchase cable clevis assembly on his boot. It looked like maybe he only had the Allen screw to back out…

The Safety signaled Deck Edge, Deck Edge told the Operator to open the valves. Another one waved off. The retract valve blew apart when the first valve was opened and the engine went to an immediate battery.

SLAM!

Burnie?

Burnie was over there wiggling like a worm in a hot skillet. Burnie had gotten hung-up in the retract and it wasn't a "ha, ha, grind a notch in your wrench" type scenario. Burn was fucked *up.*

The Air Boss was yelling over the MC to get him the hell out of the landing area, as more planes got waved off. It angered me. My friend was lying there hurt and this guy wanted to go about the business of catching airplanes. Yeah, yeah, I know…

We got Burnie hauled off.

After the Go, Ruddy had to calm me down. I had come down the passageway from the deck looking for a piece of everyone from the Engine Operator to the Boss.

It was nobodies "fault." Machines fail. Shit happens.

I was Topside PO for, like, half or three-quarters of a day. I don't know if they didn't have anyone else handy or what the deal was. I gotta' be honest with you, it was sort of cool. I was the Topside P.O.! Yeah, and I was an E-2.

They found someone else to fill the billet by the next day. Burn was released for duty in the next couple. He was banged-up and bruised, but not broken. I was happy to have him back. We worked well together.

A kid died.

He was a new Blue Shirt. They were pulling a Tommy with a tractor. A tie-down chain that had come loose from the aircraft was dangling in front of a main mount. The kid moved to swing it clear and tripped. It was at that moment the director took a check behind himself. The F-14 rolled over the kid's midriff, separating him at the torso. I wasn't there.

I'm glad I wasn't there.

Yeah, "Oops" could be a real bitch.

I was a drunken, whorin' son of a bitch the whole time we were in the Med. Other guys were off on tours seeing Pompeii or some such crap. Me? I always went to the Gut.

The Gut is where they tell you not to go. The Gut is where the whorehouses are. We hit ten different ports of call on that cruise, and I bought pussy in at least eight.

You'd always see the same faces from the boat when you were in the Gut. At first, it was kind of awkward. You'd see a guy try to act like he was lost.

Yeah, right.

After a while, it almost became like old home week.

"John! How the hell are ya? Man, I haven't seen you since, what?

"Valencia?"

Normally, I'd hit the beach by myself. There was that time Punk tagged along, though. "Tagged." Heh. That's funny.

So Punk was with me and he got this kinky idea he wanted to do one up, with me—both of us at once. Now I like nasty sex, but I haven't ever been into group sex. That time, back at the apartment with Belinda and the neighbor, I was sorta happy that the neighbor stumbled home, to be honest.

What d'ya mean, "what kinda nasty?" Leave me *some* secrets, will ya?

Punk was my buddy, though. I couldn't see any harm in doing it just to make the guy happy. Ya know? You wanna help a buddy out, right?

We got drunked-up and went whore trolling. Punk would ask them, "Both of us?" Of course, they'd agree. Then he'd hit 'em with, "At once?"

Surprisingly, none of them wanted any part of that. It was obvious Punk really had his heart set on a double, 'cause he was starting to get pissed.

That didn't help at all.

I mean, if you were a whore and some cat was animated and spitting drunk while demanding "at once!," would you be interested? Nah… me neither. Much easier money would come along any moment.

We gave up and headed back to the boat. I was feeling rather relieved about the whole thing, really.

Then we ran into that little ol' lady. She was about 5 foot tall, basically round, and had to have been at least 65 with no teeth. None that were visible, anyway.

Punk gave her the rundown, and as soon as she said "yes" I was thinking I might need another drink.

We went upstairs with her and got naked. After she washed our junk over a water bowl on the table—SOP for the biz—she directed me to the bed. She jumped down and started giving me a gum job with her wrinkly ass wriggling in the air, awaiting Punk's pleasure.

There was another granny in the room. She sat in the corner, watching a 13-inch TV. Pulling her top down, she started playing with her titties. I think she was trying to put on some kind of a show. If it was meant to make a dick hard, it wasn't working.

Punk was having a fuckin' ball! I couldn't have gotten it up if my life depended on it. It wasn't the booze; I've done up a bunch of 'em while drunker'n a skunk. It was just too fucking bizarre!

Punk blew a nut, and I gave up.

While we were getting dressed, the Primary Granny told Punk if he came back the next night she'd give him a freebie. The old hag even had a gleam in her eye. Walking back to the ship, I began to apologize to Punk for my poor performance, but he waved it off.

Punk seemed rejuvenated. That's what being shipmates is all about, I tell ya. Helping your buddy out.

I went back to solo slumming after that little adventure.

It's not just a job...

CRASHES AND TRASHES

I had just handed a Tomcat off to the Gear Puller. I had my back to it as I watched the wire retract, gauging the position of the next aircraft to trap. I could tell by the sound the rolling Tommy had his nose pointed to starboard as he powered up to give a little push to his taxi. The wire goes to battery and I'm across the Line, next plane is in the long groove. I don't hear the Tommy back off on the throttle.

What the——?

When I glanced back, my second clue that something was wrong was the Director. He was no longer directing.

He was running away.

The third was the fact that the pilot had his brakes locked, as evidenced by the tires that weren't rolling but sliding, and he was still at about 3/4 throttle.

Fuck. It's stuck.

Now I was trying to focus my attention in two places at once. I had one coming over the ramp in front of me and behind me one sliding across the deck, out of control. As I ran the hook I spied the F-14—the one with the throttle issue—running into a spotted (parked) S-3, over by the starboard catwalk.

An S-3 Viking was a large turbofan aircraft. ASW (anti-submarine warfare) was their gig. We called them "Hoovers" because of the sound of the engines. Like the vacuum cleaner. *WHOOOM.*

As I gave the retract signal, out of the corner of my eye I watched the Tommy's pilot and his RIO (radar intercept officer) eject as their nose gear dropped into the catwalk. The RIO rode in the back seat. I saw a man run right up and over another guy who was getting out of the way. As I walked back toward the Foul Line, I watched both aircraft crewmen separate from their rocket chairs. Their chutes deployed. The pilot gave us a thumbs up.

It wasn't until I looked back toward the deck that I noticed the missile. When the Tommy smacked the Hoover, a Sidewinder had fallen off and broken open.

Well, that certainly sucks.

By that point, the Boss had fouled the deck. Aircraft were waving off going into a holding pattern. I kept thinking that maybe I should go find someplace else to be, but I was also thinking I might need to hold a fire hose so I just stood there. Waiting.

The MB-5 is a big yellow fire truck. On the cab is a turret with a large nozzle that sprays foam. The MB-5 pulled up and the Crash & Smash dude manning the nozzle opened it up and let 'er rip. There hadn't been any explosion or fire. I figure it was just a preventive measure. It would have been nice if the truck had been pointed aft, rather than forward. Remember that wind over the deck? The foam blew back and covered the MB-5. It would have been comical if I hadn't been waiting for something to go *BOOM*.

I saw the EOD Team arrive. They probably appreciated that the high explosives lying on the deck weren't covered in foam. With the situation covered, I supposed it was safe to wander off and blow a bowl.

I got the crotch rot real bad. A lot of the guys would get it. I think it was from the heat and atomized chemicals. Engine operators and deck hands alike would come down with it from time to time. Most often a little bit of powder or some sort of over the counter remedy would take care of it.

Most often.

The rot? It's a rash that itches like a son of a bitch. It'll start right at the juncture of the thigh and groin, right up there, tight in the fold. From there it'll spread outwards and down. It looks like a bad-ass case of diaper rash. When a guy has a case it's obvious—he'll be digging. I had it bad. Real, real bad. The inside of my thighs were raw a third of the way to my knee. I was oozing and sticking to my drawers. It was bad.

I went to Sick Bay.

The corpsman took a look at the mess with an ultraviolet light. He said he was looking for bugs or some shit, I dunno. Whatever it was he didn't find it, or them.

"You got the rot."

I didn't bother to respond. I figured maybe, it was like, his pronouncement made it official. Obviously, I had the rot. So the

E-3 gave me a script that I promptly took to the pharmacy. All that air hitting my open flesh had put the itch into high gear. Relief was around the corner! The pharmacy mate gave me a tube of cream.

I hightailed it up to One and Two to apply the stuff. That was closer than the head or the compartment. Stone and Gator were down at the desk, getting stoned. I dropped my drawers and applied a liberal amount of the tube's contents. I yanked my dungarees back up and began to partake of the contents of their bowl.

"Son of a *bitch*!," said I.

"What?," asked Stone.

"This shit's starting to burn, man."

Gator offered, "Yeah, it's probably supposed to do that, ya know? The good shit's getting after the bad shit. It's a battle. A war."

Fuckin' Gator. Sheesh.

"Mother *FUCKER!*" That would have been me screaming. It wasn't burning any longer. It was way past burning. My balls were lying in a bed of coals and a blow torch was scorching my raw flesh.

"Fuu-uuck!"

I tripped over my dungarees as I headed down the passageway to the head. I left them there. I jumped into the shower, hoping for relief.

It didn't quite work out that way.

It felt like the water was adding oxygen to the fire between my legs.

"Oh, shit, son of a bitch, damn… damn…"

I spied a sliver of soap in the corner of the stall and managed to work up lather with it. My whole salvation consisted in the belief that the soap would cut the cream. Slowly—oh, *way* too slowly—the fire went out.

The fucksticks were still laughing at me as I hobbled off, headed back down to the pharmacy.

I tossed the tube up on the counter of the Dutch door. There was different cat behind the counter. I don't know if I looked distressed or pissed when the guy looked at me. He definitely looked to be getting ready to go defensive. I suppose my tone of voice didn't help.

"I can't use this shit, man. It flat sets me on fire. I'm talking standing in the shower with tears running down my cheeks on fire.

"That kind of fucking fire. It ain't gonna work, man."

He gave me a half-puzzled look as he picked up the tube to examine its printed contents.

"Now, *what* are you using this for?" His eyebrows had narrowed.

"The rot, man. I've got a serious case of the crotch rot and that crap right there has fried my fuckin' nuts. The inside of my thighs are singed to a crisp. That crap is *baa-ad* news, man."

He tossed it into the shitcan and picked up a small bottle of Tinactin from a shelf. It was obvious he was trying not to laugh. I wasn't humored.

"This stuff is oily," he said. "It doesn't take much. Apply it sparingly at first. You'll see. Use it three times a day."

"So what the fuck's going on here, man? What do you find so damned humorous?"

"The stuff in the tube is for athletes' foot."

I ripped the entire hydraulic system out of an F-8 Crusader. Fucked it up good.

I don't recall who, but someone on Deck Edge wanted to swap out a Go. I probably would have welcomed a break if it had been the second day out of a port. Repeatedly sprinting out to airplanes over 12-plus hours would play hell with my legs. I would normally be limping a bit the second day out from soreness. By the third, the pain would be gone. For whatever reason, we swapped out. I went to Deck Edge to pull handles.

F-8 Gators have a hitch in their git-along when they're raising the hook. It'll come right up and then drop back to the deck. As the hook begins to lift again, it'll pull itself forward a foot or so. The hydraulic system is *very* vulnerable at that point.

The plane had trapped and run out. I could see the Hook Runner clearly, as well as the hook. I could see the runner giving the "hook up" signal. I watched the hook rise, and I pulled the damned retract handle. The hook dropped and reengaged the now retracting wire. I saw that, too. Fuckin' "oops."

I saw the Hook Runner throw his hands up like "What the fuck?!" He had never given a retract signal. I have no fucking idea why I pulled the handle. None at all. No, it wasn't because I was stoned.

The Hook Runner gave "hook up" again, but it wouldn't go. It wouldn't go because there was hydraulic fluid pouring out of the aircraft.

A lot of it.

He waved over at Crash & Smash to bring the Tool. The Tool is a lever and fulcrum arrangement for raising dead hooks. Ya gotta get the hook outside of the wire, for obvious reasons.

A plane got waved off while the wire was freed.

The Hook Runner gave the plane to the Gear Puller and gave me the retract signal, for the first and only time on this trap. Both the pilot and Director had learned that the stick was dead in the plane. The pilot couldn't steer the nose gear. He couldn't do *anything*. The controls were all hydraulic. More fluid sprayed across the deck.

Another plane in the pattern waved off.

It took a few moments to get a tractor with a tow bar out to the crippled plane. They then had to fiddle around because the nose gear was pointed off at a bad angle.

The deck was still Red.

Finally they got it dragged over the Foul Line. It bled profusely the whole time.

After the Go, the Gear Officer popped into the shop to chew ass.

"What the hell happened up there?! What the hell was that?!"

I didn't see any reason to attempt some sort of bullshit story.

"I had my head up my ass. I never should have pulled the handle. I fucked up, simple as that.

"I fucked up. I have no idea why."

The aircraft sat in the hangar bay for the rest of the cruise. They craned it off when we got to the pier. I had killed it. I never heard another word.

I suppose if one could have chosen one aircraft onboard to trash, it would have been an F8 Crusader. I'm not sure what the dollar value of one was, but they were old and on the way out. Now, a $38 million Tomcat… well, I can see where the taxpayers might take issue with *that*.

We were relieved by the *Forrestal* and arrived back in CONUS April 25th of '78. I put in for my leave as I had unfinished business back in Yuma. Now, now, don't go getting all moralistic on me about that whoring thing. Hell, I wrote two or three times a week. I even drew goofy little pictures in the margins of the stationery.

I had a locker in the shop over the work bench. In the locker was my sewing gear (to add patches from each port), letter writing gear and a cassette tape player. I can't recall now why the player had to stay where it was but I know there was some reason why I was "tethered" there. After I bathed I'd go into the shop, toss some rags over the vise (it was in front of the locker), sit on it and write while I listened to tunes.

"It's Drift. He's writing a letter.

"What?"

Petty Officer 1st Class Ruddy ragged on me once because I was wearing a cut-up flight deck jersey. He threatened to write me up for destroying property or some shit. I had cut the turtle neck off it and made a V collar. I'd cut the sleeves off, too. It made for nice evening wear. I explained that I had caught the sleeve in a tow bar and rent a large rip down it.

"The shirt was no longer viable for wear on the deck, so I cut it up."

Yep. Pulled that out of my ass, right on the spot.

The whole customizing thing might have been driven more by psychological motivation than physical comfort. Wearing civilian clothing aboard ship, unless coming or going from the beach, was *verboten*. To have gone and taken a shower with an hour or so to relax before hitting the rack, a fella wanted to be … well, let's just say that some of us didn't want to "relax" in the working uniform of the day. We modified issued clothing. No, I'm not saying we made pajamas, dammit.

We made "evening wear."

FETCHING THE FAMILY WITH STONE

Stone decided to go home with me, but first I had to rent an apartment. I got one right across the street from Stone and Hairy's old place, on Diamond Springs Boulevard. After all, I knew the neighborhood.

Stone's decision to go to Yuma was based on nothing more than his penchant for adventure. His previous leaves had been to his home in the Seattle area. He had never been to the desert. He figured it was time to see something new.

He had met Belinda on her visit prior to the cruise, and the two had gotten along fabulously. He was well aware of my plans to bring my new family back by way of a drive across the United States. He knew I hadn't a fucking clue how that was going to come together.

An adventure.

He had also heard me carrying on about the price of marijuana on the Mexican border. See, when I had gone into boot camp, a kilo of weed could be had on the U.S. side for about 120 bones. Ninety on the Mexican side, but I didn't want to get into any of that. The plan was that we would return to Virginia with Belinda, the Kid, and Stone's investment.

At the airport in Chicago, we tried to smoke a doobie in a grassy area out front. The mosquitoes were so bad we had to give up halfway through. I was pissed, but Stone thought it was a fine way to begin his trek. You know how those "artistic" cats can be a bit weird sometimes?

So we landed at Sis and Chaunce's place. After the initial business of knocking off a piece, I got to hunting down Stone's pot.

Kilos weren't 120 bones anymore. Kilos weren't anywhere close to 120 bones any more. I thought that whole paraquat thing had really screwed up the market, and I told Stone so. I mean, what was I going say?

"Hey, I'm a fuckin' idiot and now I've dragged you out to the edge of hell to drive several thousand miles back home for nothing."

I couldn't say that.

I told him several things to try to make myself look less like an idiot. Stone's a real mellow cat. He always has been. Stone *oozes* mellow.

I think Stone was pissed.

Oh well, bummer. Move on.

He still likes me. He told me just the other day. We still see each other frequently. He lives a couple o' hundred miles up the road.

The next order of business was something to get us home. Being a young man of a certain age, I hadn't given it a lot of thought. It was three adults and one four year-old, from here to there. How hard could it be?

I bought a damned panel truck. A '66 Chevy panel truck. I put a clutch in it the same day I gave the nice man his money. It had a straight six in it, three on the tree. Nice big trailer mirrors. It was the delivery type with the two doors in back that opened, uh… like doors. The only side opening was one that a previous owner had cut in. It was, oh, 8" tall by 14" long. It was in the right panel. The first time I went to pull out of a parking lot, cocked slightly to the left, I figured out why it was there.

The visit was over. A small portion of the mission was accomplished (hey, I bought the damned truck, alright?), and it was time to leave.

We didn't have much with us. Me and Stone's sea bags, a few items belonging to Belinda and the Kid (Karlie); four eight-track tapes and two joints.

The trip back east was mostly uneventful. Okay, I smoked half of one of those doobies somewhere in New Mexico and about got us all killed. But it didn't quite happen. Otherwise that would have been eventful, right?

Why the hell driving while stoned would present a problem but I could run out in front of airplanes all day long while whacked… I dunno.

Belinda and Stone swapped from the only other seat to the makeshift arrangements in back. The Kid had a blast. I did most of the driving.

Oh yeah, the inner walls of the truck were bare. We stuck anything we could find between the panels and the structural ribs to try and kill the harmonic waves from the sheet metal. Though, after a while, I think I preferred the insistent rattle to another repeat of the four tapes.

We were a little tight on money, so food and overnight accommodations took priority over the music library. Stone might have picked up one other tape along the way. After all, he had about 120 smackers he hadn't planned on traveling back with. Now that I think on it, we might have landed back in Virginia Beach pretty much broke.

All of us.

The apartment became the new party pad. And we ate a shit-load of acid. Now, there you go again with your preconceived bias, prejudice and opinionated morals. It's the Kid, right?

"My God! What of the child!"

Chill the fuck out. Most of the trippin' was done over the weekends. We would be peaking long after she had gone to bed. It's not like we were amateurs. We knew what we were doing. She didn't know.

The four biggest things she remembers from that time period are her mother's friend, June, coming to visit (Stone had him some o' that); starting school; going aboard ship; and that time Gator jumped out of the closet at her when she had gone to open it.

No, I don't remember if Gator was trippin' at the time. Sheesh.

If you have any doubts you can ask her yourself. She lives right across town. Send me a self addressed stamped envelope… sorry, Kid, Pop's just trying to make a buck here.

For a period after her return, the ship sat at Pier 12. For temporary duty, I lucked out and pulled Duty Driver a few times. The Duty Driver hauls people and documents around from Naval base to base, or to the airport or wherever. Whenever I was in the neighborhood of the apartment, I'd stop in to catch a nooner, a buzz, or both.

The apartment wasn't just a "party pad," but a place where the guys in the Gear could come hang out and get away from the ship. A place to hang out in jeans and a t-shirt. The apartment complex had a swimming pool. There was always a home cooked meal in the offing.

Burnie puked spaghetti all over the porch landing one night. He never copped to it, but I know damned well it was he. Burnie always was a lightweight when it came to booze.

We kept temporary gate passes for each day of the week (they came in different colors) under the right floor mat of the truck. I couldn't get a regular base sticker, because I didn't have insurance and the panel wouldn't pass inspection.

So we faked it.

There was, like, an administrative office before the gate. Folks would go in and do the paperwork; they would be issued a temporary pass. This they would toss on the dashboard of the vehicle and gain access through the gate. We'd sit in the parking lot and wait for someone to walk out with a pass. That would give us the color of the day, and onto the dash it would go.

Probably wouldn't work so well now.

Coming out, we'd pull the pass before approaching the gate. The hope was that we'd be waved through without having to relinquish the pass. It was good to have multiples of the same color, because it sucked every time we had to give one up.

That worked for a few months. It worked until we left for the Med. Again.

Have no fear about the security of our military bases. We were professionals on a stoned course. No squids were injured during the course of operations. If you want to point fingers, blame the beer brewing companies. Friends don't let friends drunkenly violate the security of military bases.

Burp.

The damned hood blew off the truck on the way to Punk and Rob's.

They lived across the water. As we were about to enter the tunnel portion of the Bay Bridge/Tunnel thing, the latch let loose. The hood flew up, the left side came, uh, "unhinged," and the hood slid off to the right, hanging by the hinge on that side.

It wasn't dragging on the pavement. It wasn't dragging on the tunnel wall. I drove clear through to the other side that way. At my first opportunity, I stopped and pulled the other hinge loose, tossing the works in the back of the truck.

Later I straightened it out in the apartment's parking lot by running over it. I bent the hinges back with a bar. Good as new!

Pretty much. Mostly.

Some dick-weed stole Fred's stereo system out of his van while it was sitting in the same parking lot. We were pretty sure it was Hairy's girlfriend's brother. She pleaded with us not to fuck him up.

Fred let it go.

I think it was during this time when Moon was introduced to our lot. He was called Moon 'cause his last name was Mullen. There was an old comic strip named Moon Mullen. Moon was a Southern boy from Ashville. He had transferred over from the Marine Corps as an E-5. He ran a JBD up in the bow Cats.

Mine and Moon's history, really, is about when I got out. He transferred back to the Marines and got stationed at the MCAS Yuma. It was during that time that he loaned me money to buy some old motorcycle.

I also have a tattoo across the top of my right foot that Moon gave me. I had made the tattoo rig out of an aquarium air pump, amongst other things. The design on my foot is a squid. It's carrying a banner that reads, "USN Never Agin."

Oh, yeah, and he tattooed the motor numbers from my old panhead across my right wrist, too. But that all happened after this book ends.

I've only mentioned his name here because I'm sure it would hurt the man's feelings if he wasn't somewhere in here.

And 'cause I still owe him that money.

My hair started getting long.

The only two places that you have to remove your cover on a ship are the flight deck (during ops) and the mess decks. We weren't at ops and I wasn't eating on the mess decks. I was greasing my hair and then putting it up under my cover. My crewmate Rocky (the barber) would then take his clippers and do the white walls/clean neck thing. As long as it was oiled up and hidden I looked squared away. It got long enough that some gal in the apartments once asked Belinda what I did for a living. When she told her I was a squid she could hardly believe her.

"With *that* hair?"

It was when we were readying to go back out and play in the Atlantic that a most fortunate opportunity arose and gained me another few inches. Supplies had been brought aboard, but for whatever reason they hadn't been stowed. There was a stack of boxes sitting in the hangar bay about forty feet by forty feet by six feet tall. Having reconnoitered, we knew what was in the boxes: raviolis, sardines, cold cereal, soup… a fucking *gold mine*. This would be way better than having the boots steal us warm bread from the bakery.

They had an armed marine watching the goods.

In an engine room there are two removable deck plates. There's a big'un for large parts and pieces. There's also a smaller one, about a foot in diameter, for pulling cable. The purchase cable, during a rereeve, is on a spool down in the hangar bay. It gets fed into the engine room. I think it was in Number Four that it wasn't even a plate, but expanded metal. You could stand there and look into the hangar bay.

We got the Marine's attention.

While a conspirator yelled down at the grunt, making disparaging remarks about his lineage and the Corps in general, the Rat's were feeding at the opposite corner of the pile. We had a brigade going and stacked the boxes at the bottom of a ladder until we were afraid our pillaging was bit too obvious to casual passersby.

We made a hell of a haul.

Punk brought an electric wok aboard. We began going back out. I paid a cat in a parachute loft to make me a skull cap. You can wear a skull cap on deck, during ops. Mine had a chin strap.

The cat did a good job on it. On the forehead was a hook and fastener patch with a mating leather patch. You know, like on a pilot's flight suit? On the leather patch, in gold leaf, was a pair of flying shit hooks (a term of endearment for the ABE insignia) with "Capt. Drift" above and "V-2 Gear" (or some shit) below.

Parachute loft? Those are the riggers with an industrial sewing machine, so to speak. They have a large table to work on chutes. They sew nylon strapping together. I don't know. They sew stuff!

To gain access to Number One and Two starboard, you had to pass through the "paraloft." That space was only occupied when the squadrons were aboard. It was always the paraloft when they were there, though. You'd enter from the starboard passageway. Looking across the space, you'd see a small horizontal hatch at the far side.

That hatch led to One and Two starboard. You had to sit on the deck and slide to get through it. We saw the paraloft dude a lot. A cubby hole, exposed to the elevator cable well, was back in there. It was a favorite place to get stoned. Have I previously mentioned that?

He also made my topside wrench holster. Topside crew carried two wrenches. One was a large open end with the jaws bent at 90 degrees, claw like. The other was a small Allen, bent like a speed wrench. These were for the fasteners on the couplings between the CDP and purchase cable. The holster was on a nylon webbed belt that fastened with hook and loop. A piece of leather boot lace worked for a leg strap.

I mentioned Deck Edge operators knocking people down with a wire retract. They would then go to the bench grinder and grind a notch in the handle of their wrench. Yeah, it was the ol' wild, wild West gunfighter thing. I ground a few on mine. We wore our holsters in the fashion of the old gunslingers, too.

We had functioned an engine and had the wire on deck. We had yelled our warnings and were getting ready to give the retract signal. It was me that was to give it. I swung my arm, not realizing that I was standing in a bit of a loop. I was inside the line from the sheave to the center of the CDP. The wire straightened out and caught me by my heels. It knocked me down, in the bight of the wire. I rolled over on my stomach and watched the clevis/socket arrangement of the joined wires as it headed toward me. Gawdammit! Right as it got to me I did a weird push up, like you've seen people do while clapping their hands. The wire went beneath me and just clicked the steel toe of my boots as it passed.

When I went down to the shop, fucking C.O. was grinding a notch in his wrench. I told him I thought that was bullshit but he just kept grinding.

Dick.

I'm getting off track here.

My hair was getting *very* long, by Navy standards. I had mitigated any requirement to expose the wadded up greasy mess I was hiding. Man, I'd go through a tube of Brylcreem in a week. Washed out, the hair was a tad more than shoulder length. Hold that thought.

Stone and I had been getting stoned over in the blue room, on the port side. We popped into One and Two and spied a two quart can with a green liquid in it sitting on the desk. We had cotton mouth like a motherfucker. Now before you go trying to get all ahead of me, allow me to explain.

It was common for operators to scrounge up an old can from the mess decks and fill it with ice and bug juice. Bug juice being lime Kool-Aid. The machinery spaces get very, very warm. All of that friction produces a lot of heat. Bug juice and ice from the mess decks is free. An old two quart vegetable can makes a nice serving size.

Stone got to it before me and took a mouthful, immediately handing me the can for a shot. I tipped it up not realizing that that was exactly what Stone had—a mouthful. It wasn't until I had the same I knew why he hadn't swallowed. It weren't bug juice. It was a solvent. A cleaner. Some sort of fucking chemical. We spit together.

"Stone, you son of a bitch! You fucking stood there with a mouthful of that shit just so I would take a mouthful myself!"

"Drift, (spit, spit) man… I didn't want to be the lone idiot."

Stone's always had a sly way about him. I think it could have been a partial payback for that pot thing back in Yuma.

I got caught behind the Number Four jet blast deflector when an F-14 launched with afterburners. I don't know if the announcement wasn't made or if I couldn't hear it over the planes, but "no shit there I was."

I was going through my normal routine prior to walking up the deck. A Tomcat was the last to launch off the waist, Cat 4. Under a normal launch walking behind the JBD is fine. Oh, there's a little wind buffeting but it ain't no thing. An AB launch is something else entirely. I was back there when I heard him light 'em off. When the afterburners light, it sounds sort of like a muffled explosion. Boom. Not, BOOM. Well, hell. How much shit am I in?

The first thing I did was look for an avenue of escape. Hmm, fire's coming around the port side of the deflector. Yep, fire to starboard. Hell, look at that! There's fire rolling overhead, too! The steel buttons on my float coat started to burn my front side. I pulled them away from me. The topside wrench strapped to my leg was starting to cook the shit out of me. I was trying to pull that away when I decided the best move would be to just run aft and let the damned thing blow me away. I might mention, again, the flight deck is covered in non-skid. Imagine being forcefully blown across a most gnarly piece of sandpaper.

I had begun to commit when I heard, *"Bang!"* The Cat had fired. The dragon had left the premises. I walked up the deck with my holster unstrapped, holding it by the belt. The holster itself, wrench contained therein, was too hot to be close to human flesh.

And then the bastards let a 200 pound bomb go loose on me.

Again, it was either a case of I didn't hear the announcement, "Hung ordnance" or…?

I ran out on this A-6, and the son of a bitch let a bomb go! The damned weapon went skipping down the deck, just about across the toes of my boots, and off of the end of the angle.

It sort of got me excited. Pissed maybe is a better word.

The Gear Officer happened into the shop after that go.

"Hey, Lieutenant, you see that damned bomb come off? That was pretty wild, huh?"

"Yeah," he says, "it was hung ordnance."

"Hung?" I queried. "I didn't hear anything over the MC."

"I heard it on the mouse," he says.

Did I explain the mouse all-the-ready? That's the headset that puts the "important" folks on the flight deck in contact with one another, as well as the Air Boss.

I tell him nobody tells me shit and I should have a damned mouse. I note that I'm the son of a bitch standing out there getting bombs thrown at him.

He tells me, "The cost of a mouse is around $3,500. That's not an expendable amount of money."

You see now why nobody wanted to do this job?

I proposed to Belinda.

The way that whole thing went down is almost a tale in itself. I had applied for the day of our planned wedding off. It was never supposed to be a big deal, a simple justice of the peace type of thing. Still, it was the day we had planned. It turned out that after I had requested the time and it was approved, an inspection was scheduled. The division was to assemble on the flight deck wearing their summer dress uniform.

"Hey Ruddy, I'm not making the inspection tomorrow."

"Bullshit, you'll be there or you'll be U.A."

He acquiesced when I explained I was to be joined in matrimony the following day *and* that he had already approved the time. He still thought I was bullshitting him, but what could he say?

The inspection and wedding were both on a Friday. I got drunked-up early in the day and missed the formalities.

My wedding, that is.

The next day we jumped in the truck and found a retired judge that called himself a Marriage Commissioner. He performed a short ceremony and filled out the paperwork for ten bucks. He wanted twenty, but ten was all I had. His wife acted as the witness.

When I reported back on Monday no one noticed the date discrepancy on the paperwork. Or, if they did, nothing was ever said. I'd done gone and got hitched.

Belinda and the management of the apartments didn't get along. Belinda was a bit of an extrovert. She had no compunction about telling you exactly what she thought and being quite adamant about it.

There was friction.

To add more heat to the situation, the apartment was rented under me and Stone's name. There was nothing in the rental agreement about a woman and her small child.

When we once again pulled out for the Med, the manager called the coppers on Belinda expecting her to be evicted on the spot. The lease aside, shacking up was technically illegal in that place at that time. The manager had no idea we had married. When the officer arrived, he took one look at the marriage certificate and told the old gal to go pack sand.

He also took a brief, cursory look at my pipe collection. At every port I had hit, in between whorin' and boozin' I'd take the time to buy a pipe. These pipes were obviously not your regular old tobacco pipes. They were displayed on a stand.

"I see none of these have been used," says he.

"Nope, not a one," says she.

If he'd've looked on the back corner of the bottom shelf...

FULL SPEED AHEAD!

Before departing for the Mediterranean once again, I killed Fred. Well, I didn't really kill him. He was here just the other day. I mean, obviously...

We sure as shit thought I had, though.

That paraloft I was talking about earlier was also a battle dressing station. A place for first aid in the event we got blown up or the shit shot out of us.

There was a locked medical cabinet in there. Gator broke into the thing. He came bee-bopping into Number One and Two with a small metal box. In the box were four or five needled ampoules. The ampoules fit into a stainless steel frame that was included in the kit. The plunger on the frame screwed into the seal on the ampoule. The box read, "Epinephrine."

Now, this was before personal computers and search engines putting a world of information at your finger tips. We had a dictionary. Webster's said Epinephrine was artificial adrenaline. Sweet. We had, like, pharmaceutical speed.

We hauled ass back to One and Two.

I tied off and pumped a few CCs of the stuff into a vein in my arm. Fucking rush! Wow! I was still getting my shit together when Fred grabbed the tie and wrapped it around his arm.

"You fucking pussy. The whole ampoule is the dose. Why else would they be packaged like that?

"Pump that whole son of a bitch in here!"

I had about half of it in him when he turned green. I'm talking The Hulk Green. I was still pushing on the rig when he fell out. I sprayed Epinephrine all over the damned place. Blood dripped from his arm. Fred was green and lying on the deck, doing the fish dance. The convulsions looked a little more serious than passing out from a whopper hit off o' the pot pipe. Then he lay there a moment and just sort of vibrated. And then he was just laying there, still. The tie was still on his arm.

Shit-oh-dear. I've done gone and killed Fred.

We split. We were scared. We regrouped in another space.

Gator asked, "Are we sure he's dead? Nobody took his pulse."

"He wasn't breathing, man," I answered. "Christ, he still had the tie on his arm! The motherfucker's toast.

"Fred's fucking fried, man!"

Stone was calmer.

"Okay, we need to slow down and think about this," he said. "So Fred's laying there dead. How does that come back on us?"

"Well, he's not even in V-2," I said, "for one.

"People know of our association. Finding a dead Tractor King in an engine room is going to have someone asking questions."

"Fuck," cried Gator. "I ran off and left the box of dope!

"My fingerprints are all over that shit."

I said, "We need to go back and tidy up. If we toss Fred over the side, with something heavy attached, he'll be well below the surface before the watch could spot him."

"Drift," Stone asked reasonably, "how the hell are we supposed to get a dead man from One and Two out to the catwalk without being seen?"

"Uh, well, uh…"

"At the very least we have to go back and make the box with the speed go away," Gator pointed out, obviously still worried about his connection to the evidence. "The rest of it… I dunno."

We agreed. We had to take care of the damning evidence. Maybe we could play dumb about poor, dead Fred. No one could break though our united resolve.

"We don't know. How could we know? We don't know shit. I didn't do it, *maaaan!*"

Turned out, Fred wasn't dead after all. He was sitting up with the tie lying on the deck between his legs. Though drool was running off of his chin (I figured it was drool, as I didn't see anything that really looked like puke), his color looked a lot better.

Or at least not all the way green.

"What a fucking rush!," he screamed. "Son of a *bitch*, my head feels like it's gonna *explode!*"

He thought about it for a second, then frowned. "I'm not doing any more of *that* shit! That shit's fucked *up*, man. I don't want *any* more o' that.

"Where'd you guys go?" We offered him a hand up. "Nah, that's cool. I'll just sit here another minute."

Gator threw the box and dope over the side. We kept Fred.

I had an interlude with the Admiral. The *America* was a flag ship. That means (I think) that the guy I had a brief discussion with was the same guy running the whole task force show. Not just the *America*'s show, but that of every vessel that was in support.

See, a carrier is an adversarial killing machine, but all you have to do is trash out that flight deck to knock it out. The flight deck must be protected.

Must be.

Because if a carrier can't launch her aircraft, she's nothing more than a big chunk of floating metal. As long as she *can* launch, she is bad fucking news. That flight deck must remain intact. That protection involves at least a half a dozen other naval vessels, all designed to take out missiles or aircraft or any other damned thing that might compromise the carrier flight deck. There's always a sub out there somewhere, too.

The Admiral was the guy who ran that show, I'm pretty sure.

Between ops, fellas would jog on the deck. Enlisted, officers, whomever—folks would run. I was changing out a grease fitting on a topside sheave when I noticed this older cat stop over on the starboard side and kneel to the CDP purchase cable connection point. I watched him a moment. He reached out with his hand and touched it. Lives depended upon that connection.

I walked over and said, "Hey, how the hell are ya? You lose something down there?"

"No," the old boy says, "I just never stopped to see how this was done."

"The CDP fitting slips into the purchase cable, as you see. It's all held together by that pin which in turn is held in place by... who the fuck *are* you?"

The grey-haired gent smiled and said, "Jones."

I was about to make some smart-assed remark like, "Yeah, and I'm Smith," when I got a little niggling in the back of my mind. He caught my look.

"Admiral Jones," he smiled.

Shit-oh-dear.

I was about to give Flag the boot. "Flag," as in when you hear *ding-ding-ding-ding*, "Flag arriving."

That flag. The damned Carrier Group Eight Commander. I popped to. It wasn't a conscious reaction. I suspect brainwashing.

"My apologies, sir! That connection is integral to the safe operation of the equipment. My concern was its security."

"As you were, sailor. I understand completely."

He had already stood. He smiled again and resumed his running. I swear I heard him laugh as he was gaining speed.

It was while I was living in the apartment that I discovered my cock is pierced. Now, you might be thinking, "How the hell does a man one day suddenly discover he has a pierced dick?

"Isn't that something a guy should, well, you know… *know*?" For the initial portion of the answer, I think you'd have to refer clear back to Chapter One, second paragraph. I was about seven years old when The Evil Stepmother had me baptized Catholic, had my tonsils and adenoids removed and got me circumcised. The surgical procedures were all done in one whack, so to speak. She was a real go-getter.

The sutures used for the foreskin removal were of the self dissolving kind. How many people out there have ever experienced stitches in their wanker? A handful? It ain't no picnic, I'm here to tell ya. So I had gone eleven or so years with these Frankenstein scars around the head of my pecker. I hadn't ever really paid them much attention. I have a shitload of scars. It's not like I inspect them on a regular basis.

I was in the shower, washing my junk, and for some reason a couple of spots caught my attention. A particular portion of the scar was a hole. There appeared to be a match to it, not but maybe a half-inch around the circumference.

Hmm.

Still contemplating the holes in my dick, I emerged from the shower and spied one of the Ol' Lady's earrings hanging off a rack. It was a three inch-long dangly. Hmm. I took the loop and placed it at the one hole. I gently pushed. It popped out of the other!

Fuckin' A! Fish on, baby!

I danced in front of the mirror with it for a few moments. I found it pretty damned wild. Heh! Look at that! I went into the bedroom to share my new discovery.

She was standing near the bed when I came out of the bathroom. I stood there naked, my legs slightly parted, her earring dangling from my Johnson. I didn't have to point it out. It was pretty obvious there, swinging gently from side to side.

She went pale. For a moment I thought she was going to pass out. I was standing there giggling and jiggling. She was mortified. She thought I had gone into the head and pierced my dick, just like that. I mean, with all o' that acid we were eating…

We were mean to boots. It was standard procedure that all the E-2s and non-rates went TDY to either the laundry or the mess decks before going to their respective departments for full duty. It's kind of a slave labor thing, but different.

You'd come across guys headed for V-2 on the mess decks. Seldom would you see one sweating away in the laundry. Oh, sometimes they'd come snooping around to say "hey" and get a handle on where they were going. For the most part, it was the dish washers you were exposed to, so to speak. It actually worked well that way. A guy working in the laundry didn't really have anything we wanted. Those on the mess decks did.

Food. I'm talking steaks and shit, man. Delivered to One and Two. Gravy train like a *motherfucker*, man!

There was one particular young man… we called him Junk-yard Baby after we learned he was full of aftermarket parts. Yeah, I don't think he told the recruiter about the plastic plate in his head.

He was slopping mystery meat on trays when I noticed the fly-ing shithooks on his shirt (no, I'm not going to call it a blouse!), those being the insignia of aviation boatswain mates. He said he was headed for the Gear.

I asked him if he wanted to work on the flight deck. Said I was the Hook Runner, and I had some serious pull. Said that when he reported, I could get him on Deck Edge right off the bat. Said it would cost him…

Several times a week, Junkyard brought us everything from piping hot T-bone steaks to pizza. Now and again, he'd bring hot loaves of fresh baked bread to the shop. Junkyard was kissing some serious ass.

Stone kept telling me I was being mean, but don't think he wasn't scarfing down the steak, too. We worked this poor kid until we about broke him. When the day came that he reported to the shop, I just happened to be there.

He dropped his sea bag, eyes bright. He had arrived at what would become his home for the next several years. He was being greeted by his buddies from the flight deck!

"Drift!," he exclaimed. "I'm here, man!

"Finally!"

I snuffed out my cigarette and picked up my cup of coffee, brushing past him as I headed for the passageway.

"Who the fuck are you, boot? I don't fucking know you!"

Behind me I could hear Stone, "Drift, that's fuckin' cold, man. That's just wrong."

Junkyard went to a sheave damper. I did take him up the Foul Line, though.

It got to be a ritual with me. I'd be mean to the bastards, then take them up on deck, let them have a taste. I'd talk to their PO and Burnie (like Burnie gave a shit), and get it set up. I'd tell the boot to never get more than five feet from me, except when I was doing my thing.

"If I point at the deck then I'm telling you to stand there," I'd tell them. "Don't move until I tell you to—unless if you don't, something is going to maim or kill you."

I'd stop at Crash & Smash on my way up the line and inform them I had meat with me. I'd park the boot and walk on up to the Puller and advise him, too. I did it for two reasons. The first being that I'd let these guys know we had a variable in our midst. The other was so they'd be sure to watch him run on the first trap.

They always did. Always. Every fucking one.

I'd stand at my spot with the guy placed about five feet starboard of me. Me between him and the Foul Line. About the time I'd start to sprint to port, to the plane, I'd catch them out of the corner of my eye headed to starboard at top speed.

When the go was over, you would have thought I'd taken 'em on a trip to Disneyland. The adrenaline would be pouring out of them and their mouth wouldn't shut. They'd be jabbering about what a rush it was. Sometimes I'd have a hard time shaking them off after that. Cling-ons.

We got in trouble for mooning a Russian trawler.

The damned thing had been at our starboard for a couple of days. It was only a few miles off. No net ever went into the water. When we turned, it turned. It didn't take a heap of smarts to know we were being observed. So, we thought we'd give them something to look at, namely, our assholes and ball sacks.

The six of us lined up and dropped 'em, shining our white flesh and stinking brown eyes across the waters. We then turned, stood and gave them the finger. It was a simple, cold gesture to a cold enemy.

After the Go, the El-Tee stopped in the shop to chew us out, sorta. He had a hard time keeping a straight face as he asked what the hell made us feel we were qualified to state U.S. diplomatic policy. It was plain to see the guy was reluctantly doing as he was told. We did our job by replying with the required, "Yes sir! No sir," as applicable. And then we mooned *him*.

No, not right then. That wouldn't have worked a'tall.

The Gear officers were always pilots. I think the one before this was a C-2 pilot. This one maybe an A-7 jockey? Something like that. I wonder if being a Gear or Cat officer was like going to the mess decks or laundry for the non-rates? It was obviously a temporary duty, and a pilot surely wouldn't want to babysit a bunch of drug-rattled gear rats.

They had to keep their credentials up to date. That meant flying an airplane on and off of the flight deck. They did that in *Miss America*, a twin radial, piston-driven prop plane used for Carrier On Deck deliveries of mail and personnel. Yeah, it would blow fire out of the exhaust when the ignition switch was closed on start-up, but it didn't need a cat to launch. The angle deck was plenty long enough. So, the Cat and Gear officers would routinely pilot *Miss America*.

Our El-Tee was in the pilot's seat as they sat on the fantail running up. The Cat officer was preparing to tell him to let the brakes go when we let go. All six of us, same as before, balls and brown eyes. He never said a word.

On March 13, we sailed for the Med.

Back to the Big Lake

Crazy Shoe was pulling gear. He was certifiably fuckin' nuts. The only time I ever went into the Blue Shirt locker, flight deck level at the bottom of the tower, Shoe had invited me. We were waiting on a tanker and the weather was miserable. For whatever reason, the plane was twenty minutes to a half hour out. Crazy Shoe invited me to their break room.

The space was the width of the tower with a hatch port and starboard, and it measured about ten feet forward to aft. A padded bench ran along both the forward and aft bulkheads. The only people in the space were me, Shoe, and the Flight Deck Chief. I took a seat aft and Shoe took one on the forward bulkhead. A duct about thirty inches in diameter ran from the overhead through the deck and separated Shoe and the Chief, each to their own side.

I watched Shoe pull out his hash pipe. I'm thinking, *no fucking way*. He put it to his lips and fired it up, taking a big hit. He stuck the pipe and lighter back into his pocket and exhaled into the manual inflation tube on his float coat. And then he winked at me.

I looked over at the Chief and smiled. Chief said something about the shitty weather, having no idea whatsoever about what had just transpired.

You haven't seen shit yet.

A C-2 trapped. You know what a C-2 is, a Hummer? Okay, how about a "Hawkeye?" That was the propeller plane that carried a radome on its back. Take off the dome, strip out the fancy electronics and you've got yourself a cargo plane. That's a C-2.

I didn't care much for the C-2s or E2-Cs. Oh, it wasn't the trap. It was those damn props. At night it was common for them to spot, after trapping, with their nose right on the Foul Line. Right about where I would be standing. And those props would be going round and round, just a humming.

I would repeat in my head, *If anything goes wrong, do not go that way. If anything goes wrong...* I did not care for those propellers.

So much so that some time after my discharge, it would still affect me. Unbeknownst to me, my father-in-law installed a ceiling fan in his living room. I walked in and caught the "prop" out of the corner of my eye and dove to the carpet. As soon as my chin slid across the pile I realized...

You should have seen the look on everyone's face. They still looked at me funny, even after I explained.

Back to the trap, then.

It didn't start out as anything special. He had trapped One or Two and had started his run-out. It wasn't until the pilot decided he wanted to once again become airborne that things got interesting.

Yeah, the son of a bitch tried to fly. With his hook firmly engaged in the Gear, he was still gaining altitude. This was one of those instances where I thought my chances were better hitting the deck rather than running. I had already begun moving toward him when he had left the deck. I really didn't have any place to go. I dove, trying to be the smallest target I could possibly be.

There was no way this could be good.

I watched him come back to the deck, hard, nose first. Hard enough that it destroyed the nose gear. Parts and pieces were being blown all over the fucking place.

Small. Be small.

What really caught my attention was the intact wheel, with tire. It came careening out of the debris field. My head turned as I watched it pass in front of me. I could tell it was going to take a bounce once it was by.

That's when I spied Shoe. He was just standing there. It was obvious the bounce would be in his general location.

Shoe had a moment, while the tired wheel was still approaching, to shake out his imaginary bullfighter's cape. He was standing, his feet together in a classic pose, the "cape" held out beside him as the wheel bounced on the deck, directly below and between his hands. Shoe gave a 360 degree swirl.

"Toro!" Then he looked at the tower and gave the internationally recognized hand signal for "who gives a fuck." That would be a vigorous back and forth motion with a fist, from the groin. He then strolled off toward the Blue Shirt locker.

Certifiable, I'm tellin' ya.

We had an unexpected division inspection. Most of the time those were done just to fuck with you. I couldn't really see any other reason.

The uniform for inspections was generally dungarees or utilities. They'd take a look and make sure your name was stenciled and legible. I had one complete work uniform that met those requirements. I never wore it, except for inspections.

They'd take a look at your mustache or beard. More or less an overall look-see. It was after we had mustered that I flashed. Before the walk through , but after the muster, the order was given, "Uncover... Two!" I wasn't expecting a haircut inspection.

Yeah. I'm busted.

The next thing I knew, some cat grabbed my arm from behind and swapped places with me. This happened several more times before they had shuffled me back to the port catwalk, down which I disappeared.

See, my whole hair thing had become some sort of rebellious rally back in the aft V-2 berthing compartment. When I was at the rack, toweling off from a shower, fellas would keep watch just as if someone was blowing a bowl at their rack.

The way it worked was, if someone "heavy" stepped in from the port or starboard passageway the watch would yell, "Foul deck!" It would be as an echo, "foul deck, foul deck, foul.."

Once the Master at Arms told us if they heard anyone call a foul deck they'd grab them up on the spot. We started yelling, "Popcorn. Peanuts!"

They gave up.

Before every grease job, I'd have to pull the towel off of my head several times so I could show someone how long it had gotten. I dunno. It's hard to explain. It was like I was flying everyone's freak flag.

The near-bust got me to thinking. My hair was *way* beyond "see the barber in 24 hours, or I'll write you up." I could braid the shit. I hadn't had a decent meal in some time, the mess decks being *verboten*. Guys would bring me up stuff when I asked, but most of my meals came out of a can of something warmed in the wok. It wouldn't surprise me if someone was to tell me there were still tins of sardines in the One and Two desk drawer when the ship was sunk. I wanted to go to the mess deck, sit and eat a real meal.

Wasn't that what this whole damned adventure was supposed to be about? Eating three meals a day. Every day. The Navy feeds well aboard ship. Hell, I've had steak and lobster! The lobster was of the Rock variety and the steak petit sirloin… but still. Smuggled sliders weren't getting it. It was just before I reached up for the Brylcreem that I made my decision.

I put the word out that The Hair was going. The guys were disappointed, but they were well aware of the sacrifices I had made. I also decided I wouldn't let it go quietly. I owed that to the crew. There had to a climax of some sort. You owe that to your buddies when they've supported you, right?

Something mechanical was going on with Three Starboard. I don't know what it was. The maintenance crew had been awakened early. My chief, CPO Penn, had been in there along with "Nuts & Bolts," the Maintenance warrant officer. Three Starboard was down the passageway, between the compartment and the shop. I put together a scheme with Rocky, the Gear's resident barber.

I toweled my hair and combed it out. I even had it pretty much dried out as I started down the passageway. When I stopped at the sheave damper and popped my head in through the hatch, my hair fell over my shoulders.

"Hey, Penn! How the hell are ya? Motherfucker's all FUBARed, huh?"

At first, he was irritated by my tone of voice and obvious disrespect. He looked over with a word, or words, on his lips… and froze. Penn had a tendency to stutter when he got excited. What he was looking at left him entirely beyond that. He couldn't make any sound at all for a couple of seconds. When CPO Penn finally started to get a handle on it, he initially sounded like an old model T starting up, "Ta, ta, pa, ta, ga, ge, ge—

"*Get* the fuck out of my passageway!"

See, Penn had just made Chief. He was my Chief. I was his ass standing out there for everyone to see. My being found out wouldn't be a good thing for a new Chief.

"Sure, Penn. I'll meet you at the shop."

Rocky's clippers were going before I sat in the chair. He ran 'em straight over my skull, just like they do in boot. It was all gone in literally less than 30 seconds. Penn came through the door (it was a door, not a hatch) like a puffer fish in blush: red, and under extreme pressure.

He began to blow.

While he was in the midst of telling me about how he was writing me up, I removed my cover, gave my skinned head a scritch, and asked him what in the world he was carrying on about.

"Hair?," I asked. "It's plain to see, Chief Penn, that I haven't got any.

"I haven't the foggiest what you're getting all excited about."

The 15 or so guys in the shop couldn't stifle their laughter. Penn left a bit humiliated. I don't recall now why being mean to Penn was okay. I do seem to remember that everyone thought he had it coming. I'll be damned if I can remember why, though. I know that in some fashion I scored one for the team.

I did go to the mess decks and pig out, but I didn't quit wearing my skull cap. It turned out to be quite functional.

Speaking of doors and hatches; it was years after my separation before I flashed on this: All the passageways on 0-3 level that led to weather decks had a hatch. There were hatches leading to decks above and below. Hatches led to all of the sheave dampers. All of the other doors on the 0-3 were just that—not hatches, but doors. Hell, it was only a curtain on the port and starboard of the berthing compartment.

That makes sense, right? You want to secure one level from another. The interior needs be secure from the exterior. That is why the dampers were hatched, because of the deck penetration for the cable. Of course, that meant that a sheave damper operator would be exposed to any biological or nuclear attack. That space was sealed, but behind him. I just thought I'd take a moment to point that out.

I didn't do a bunch of boozing and whoring this cruise. Oh, I'd like to say it was because I was a married man, but I don't know how much truth there would be to that.

I just didn't have the money. I was sending everything but soap and cigarette money back to Virginia Beach. There were people there to feed, rent and utilities to pay. I would cash my check at Disbursing, then buy money orders at the post office. The eagle shat (as we called it) on the first and the fifteenth of every month.

The next letter I wrote following payday would contain the bones. I don't know how I managed to have three separate money orders at one time.

I kept a stand-up locker in Number Three. Why I had been taking care of my financial business from there, I don't know (though it would be a base for another business, at a later time), but apparently I was. Once I went bebopping into Three and Stretch asked me to look in my locker to see if anything was missing.

Let me tell you about Stretch, just a bit, before I go on.

Tall and skinny, as you'd imagine, Stretch was a mellow kind of a guy unless he got wound up. Then it would be all about a fit.

He would blend Tang and instant tea and other stuff for a hot water drink. It was really good. He'd give you a spoonful for your cup now and again; called it something-or-other Dragon. Said it had a "boost."

Stretch was always looking for a way to make an easy buck. He sold a bit of hash, now and again, but not being a doper himself I don't think he thought it a good fit for him even though he never smoked into his profits. He was the kind of guy who sold his cigarette punch card.

Over there they gave you a ration card. Each time you bought a carton at the ship's store, your card got a punch. At sea, a carton was only $2.50, by the way. You were only allowed so many punches. The purpose was to keep down the traffic in black market smokes.

They'd give you a look-over when you left the boat. Four packs of smokes would be pushing it. A carton? No fuckin' way would they knowingly let you hit the beach with that. I used to routinely take what I figured would be an extra pack so I could tip the whore with it. I've always been a classy son of a bitch that way.

Stretch made most of his money loan sharking. He had the one-for-ten program going. That's pretty decent for a shark, if you ask me. That was how the interest ran: ten bones for every one hundred. He didn't let cats get in deep, and he wouldn't loan more than a C-note to a new customer. Stretch was a businessman.

Three of my money orders went missing. They were blank, other than the dollar amounts. They were as good as cash, just like folding green money. The damage to me equaled around $500.00. This would be a bad hit. This would be a catastrophic financial fuck-up.

Shit-oh-dear.

"Three money orders are gone," I sighed, and Stretch handed them to me.

"You left them on *top* of the locker, Drift. If anyone else had found them…"

Stretch was an extremely honest businessman. That was one of the incidents in my life that left a mark on me.

Thank you, Stretch.

I got blown down once, and got my ass chewed for it. They turned one on me when I was running one. Burnie got after me and then wouldn't believe me when I tried to tell him it just happened.

I went to run a hook and the bastards turned the last plane off the angle on me. It hit me at the shoulders. I was already sprinting out to the trapping aircraft and I knew it would bowl me over. Being the spry, healthy young man I was at the time, I did a shoulder roll under the wing of the trapping aircraft. Then I popped up and did my stuff. T'weren't a thing, really. Not until the Go was over anyway. I could already see Burnie was pissed when I got within ten feet of him.

"Drift, I get my ass chewed by the Boss, because of you, at least once a week. Now, I can see you getting caught out by hook skips. I can see a lot of things, but what I'm not going to get chewed for is fucking *acrobatics*.

"Catching wings is one thing. Flips? No. *Fucking. Way.* Don't do it again."

"Burn! The fuckers blew me down, man. I got *blown!*"

As of a few months ago from this writing, Burnie still doesn't believe me. He still thinks I was trying to add another level of excitement to running hooks.

Dammit, Burn… I got blown!

I received a letter from Belinda. Within the envelope were her written words, about half a dozen pubic hairs (at my request) and a hit of window pane acid. That was her surprise for me.

Previously, Belinda had sent me a photo of her scantily clad body. Her tits were bared in it. I took the photo and taped it to the overhead of my rack. I had a bottom rack at the time, so it wasn't visible unless you were snooping around. Bottom racks lay right on the deck. When you weren't in it, it was to be lifted up and attached to the bottom of the middle rack. That freed the deck for swabbing and such. The racks were set up in three tiers: bottom, middle, top. The row ran three or four long from the bulkhead (Number Three was on the other side) to berthing compartment passageway. It was the same beside you, with a passageway between the racks.

So, if your rack lay head against the bulkhead and you had a middle rack, there would be one above and below you, one beside you, and one at your feet. Personal hygiene was of great importance. Farting was dealt with on a per-violation basis.

Lying on the mattress, the distance to the rack above was my forearm and hand with the index finger pointed. The elbow would be on the mattress, finger touching the bottom of the rack overhead. Yeah, we made partitions out of anything we could find. Everyone called his rack "my house."

I don't recall who he was, but there was one guy with a top rack that had a return duct running right above it. He had breached the duct just a tad, so that you could sit up there (after hitting the head for a shower; remember "evening clothes"?) and smoke hash. The vent would suck up the smoke. And, of course, there was the always-present watch.

"Popcorn! Peanuts!"

Another fella had tapped a cold air supply over his rack. When it was cooking out, he could close his rack curtains and chill his house while he slept.

So, I had this photograph taped up there.

I came to my rack and it was gone. I figured there was only one motherfucker...

That would be the worthless, piece of shit no-load they had compartment cleaning. I don' recall this guy's name, but he was a real piece of work—worthless as the proverbial tits on a boar hog. I didn't know he'd taken it, but I was pretty sure.

I went to see him.

"Look, motherfucker, that photo you stole from me is my god-damned wife."

He started acting like he didn't know what was going on. You know the drill, "Who, me?"

"It's like this, you son of a bitch: I'll be back in an hour. If that picture isn't back, I'm tossing your worthless ass over the fuckin' side."

I grabbed him up a little bit to make my point. I came back around a half hour later and found it lying on my mattress. I found him in the head. He was cleaning a shower. That was most fortuitous. The mess went right down the drain.

No muss. No fuss.

Regarding the contents of the letter, or actually the envelope:

So I took those pubes and twisted them up like a toothpick. I then placed them in the corner of my mouth and walked around with them in that fashion, even removing them when I spoke and gesturing with them as one might a toothpick or piece of straw. I was looking for the shock value.

"What the hell is that hanging out of the corner of your mouth, Drift?"

"My Ol' Lady's pubes, man. No, really... see?"

That was only good for a day. A low mumble of "that shit ain't right" was about all I got, come the end of it. I think I ended up taping those below the photo.

I ate the acid, then ran hooks.

I told Burnie when I was going to do it. I mean, everyone knew I'd gotten the hit in the mail. It might have been Cowboy who said I didn't have a hair on my ass unless I ate the sumbitch and *then* grabbed a few wings. Cowboy had a habit of questioning the follicle count in one's butt crack.

"You want a rush, motherfucker? You think you're some sort of shit-hot fuckin' hook runner? Eat that hit of acid and run some fuckin' hooks, Cap'n Fuckin' Drift. Yeah, that's what I thought.

"You ain't got a hair on your ass."

I was a kid. I put it on my tongue right then and there. Everyone knew I had to. Everyone.

And then I ran hooks.

I started to get off during the first go. I was having a problem keeping my face straight. I was laughing at airplanes. After, I assured Burnie I was good. No problems; I had control. I started peaking on the Go after. Have you ever tried to describe an acid trip to someone?

I mean, you can talk about tracers and walls melting and all of that crap. What I've never been able to do, nor heard done, was describe the inside of the mind during the peak. Not the walls. Not the pretty colors. The fucking *mind*.

I was tripping my ass off and working one of the most dangerous jobs on the face of the planet. I knew it. It was okay, because I was in control. The whole shebang was under my control. I kept every aircraft moving on the deck of the carrier filed in my mind.

183

I had every airborne aircraft filed in a separate section. Another part—the forward, "right now" part—I devoted to the one that was about to trap Number Three… and I would reach out, grab its wing, and stop it.

It was my world. I was an all-powerful being.

Pretty damned lucky I'm not a dead sumbitch, eh? Old Burn might have helped me out there.

After the Go, I walked over to Burnie on our way to the catwalk, headed for the shop.

"I'm catchin' 'em, Burn."

"Yep," he says. "That's what we do, man. We catch airplanes."

"No, Burn, I mean *I'm* catching 'em! It's such a fucking rush!"

"Lift your goggles, Drift. I said *lift your fucking goggles!*

"Christ on a stick! That's it, I'm pullin' you. You're outta here… off the deck!"

"Burn!"

"You're gone, man. I'm not even sure the lights are on. Go hide under the barricade until you're done peaking. I'll let you back on *after* you peak. Got me? Two recoveries?

"I'll move some people around, tell 'em you've got the shits or something. I'll check on ya. Go fucking hide."

As it turned out, my nest under the table was an excellent place to trip your balls off, so to speak. Yeah, I missed two recoveries. It was *good* acid. I'm thinking Burnie could tell just by looking at me.

Not one swinging dick gave me a bit of shit for getting pulled. Not one.

Yeah, that would have been the second "bye." You'll recall the first was Burn and C.O.'s little mescaline incident with the burning tractor.

Even-steven, then?

Two men died. They were in an S-3 Viking and ejected somewhat inverted. It was a freak incident. Why is it that's always the "freak" incident when someone dies? I wasn't on deck at the time. It was one of the rare times when we had enough crew for two full shifts, possibly with one or two guys on both the port and starboard side bouncing between sheave dampers.

The plane approached from starboard to port. There was some question about why they weren't waved off or if they were, why they didn't go around.

It was a training flight. There were only two in the plane, not the usual four. They trapped Number Four with their angle of attack too far to port, and ran out of flight deck at the forward port catwalk. When the plane's port main mount went in the hole, the aircraft fell off the deck.

The pilot pulled "Eject." He and the other fella ricocheted off the hull of the ship like pinballs made of meat, and slid down into the ocean.

The plane stopped falling with its cockpit in the water, hanging off Number Four's CDP like a bobber on a fishing line. The purchase cable was tangled through the various grey iron of *America*.

The boat hauled hard to port to float the aircraft off the line. That plane sank to the bottom of the sea.

Those men's bodies were never recovered.

We rereeved Number Four.

You got terribly dirty working on the deck. It wasn't just the grease and goop from handling wires. There were fuel spills. There was jet exhaust. Standing behind jets is nasty, man. There's like this coat of kerosene on everything, including you. If it weren't for the non-skid painted across the deck, it would have been like an ice rink.

The air was terribly bad when we had those F-4s aboard. We had a Marine Detachment doing their carrier qualification. Why the hell does everyone think they need to land on a damned aircraft carrier? The Brazilians, the Marines…

The planes ran way dirty. Every time they launched off the bow, you'd be short of breath and your eyes would tear up. Phantoms damned sure weren't a wing-grabbing plane, the wing being within the trunk of man height.

Nope, I'm not running out in front of that.

Not even on acid. The way the landing gear was set up, the exhaust hit low. Instead of getting hit along the shoulders by jet wash, the fuckers tried to take your feet out from under ya. I didn't like 'em. That might be why I found some joy when the jockey launched with his brakes locked. Yeah!

Heh. Snork.

He got the standard Phantom send-off from the waist. The plane got flung, but his tires never turned once. They blew apart, sending crap all over the place.

Bye-bye, Phantom. Maybe you should go try to land in, like, Rota, Spain. Not here.

He didn't come back. I'm guessing the aircraft mounts sustained just a little bit of damage when he landed on a foamed asphalt runway on the mainland.

Before we went to the mess decks (the topside crew always ate together, with Punk), we would hit the shop and wash up. "Wash up" meaning the hands and arms, halfway up the forearm. A splash on the face, maybe.

Then down we'd go, swaggering with our "pistolas" swinging from our thighs, our clothes covered with grease, grime and kerosene from neck to toe.

This time, there was a pretty good line. After we picked up our trays, it was obvious that the tables were full and we'd have to break up. I spied a three-spot table over by a bulkhead. There were two cats sitting there, leaving me the open hole. I swooped on it. After the required salutation of "hey," I commenced to eating. With the line and all, there wasn't a lot of time between Gos. I was there for the food, not social hour.

C'mon, you can't think I'd forgotten about the three squares? I hadn't done *that* much dope.

Pretty quick, though, I noticed these guys were wearing starched dungarees. Their names were stenciled on their shirts as though by a pro. Their hair was very 4-0.

These are some squared away sailors… they probably work in Dispersing.

I was still cool with all of that. We all had our jobs, right? It was the aroma of attitude that finally caught my attention.

Those fucking dicks were put off because some greasy, kerosene-stinking son of a bitch had sat at their table. Man, I swear these pussies were, like, wrinkling their noses and shit. It started to chap my ass. I wasn't exactly sure what I was going to do to put these little fucks in their place until I spied the cockroach.

Oh yeah, there were roaches on the boat. No, this isn't like the chicken thing. There were bats in the belfry, so why not roaches on the mess decks?

It wasn't a big roach. If I had to guess, I'd it call it a Medium-Long. It was crawling across the bulkhead against which the table sat, right next to my chair. I speared it with my fork and popped it into my mouth, then took another scoop off my tray without missing a beat.

It fucked dudes *up*, man!

Damn, I so wish the fellas could have witnessed the whole thing. Dudes stopped eating. They just stopped. They laid their utensils down. They looked at each other. They got up, grabbed their trays and left. I finished shoveling in what I could before the next Go. I found it a very satisfying meal.

Crunchy, too.

The Master at Arms caught J.J. smoking hash over on the port side. They tried to charge him with some sort of distribution thing, but that sort of fell apart because he had all six grams in the pipe he was pulling on.

J.J. was like that. You had to watch him whenever he was handed a pipe. He would huff that sucker dry, with smoke bellowing from his nostrils. J.J. wasn't quite right in the head.

They brought on a kilo of hash in the Captain's gig, and we cut it up in Three Starboard. Yeah, a fucking kilogram. It was sweet the way that was done.

Most ports don't have large enough facilities to bring a carrier to the pier. In some cases, I would guess that even if it were physically possible, it wouldn't be in the best interest of the Navy nor the port to do so. We sat out in the harbor or bay, going back and forth to the beach in what we called "liberty launches."

The Captain had his own gig.

They had copped the dope and stashed it on his gig. When the carrier was readying to get under way, the launches and gigs are lifted aboard ship and stowed in the hangar bay.

Heh.

So we had this kilo of hash, and our mission was to cut all but a couple of ounces into grams. That's a shitload of grams. It took us a while.

We didn't have scales, but we knew what a chunk that would go for ten dollars should look like. That would have been about the size of your index fingernail, cubed—give or take. We called that a gram. Our tools were a couple of candles and some butter knives. We had this big-assed chunk of blond looking cheese that we cut into just short of a thousand pieces. That took a couple of hours, and it was a bit smoky in there.

We got beyond stoned. It was like our brains were saturated. They could absorb no more. There was no point in loading the bowl any longer. None.

Knife to candle… knife to hash… wrap… knife to candle… knife to hash…

"What? Huh? Did you say something?"

I peddled a shitload of it myself. It got to be a pain in the ass.

I had a Snickers box full of "grams." I mean, a Snickers box like the one the candy bars are in on store shelves, near the checkout. A bit bigger than a shoe box, maybe? That was a whole bunch of hash to move. I was doing this gig where I was running out in front of airplanes for a goodly number of hours in the day, plus selling hash. It got to be a pain in the ass.

Out of necessity, I started an honor system. The dope peddling seriously interfered with my time on the mess decks. I no longer had anything of importance in my standup locker in Number Three, other than my dress uniforms. I took a spanner wrench and purposely jacked the lock so that even though it appeared to be locked, a very gentle nudge would set the shank free. The box and book were already sitting on the top shelf.

I'd come down off of the deck and be scrubbing my paws, getting ready to go have a bite when some cat would approach and whisper, "I want two grams, man."

"Cash or payday?"

A lot of business was done "'til payday" or, as we called it, "when the eagle shit." You knew where everyone lived, and they weren't going anywhere for years. A cat was either good for it or he wasn't. It didn't take long to know where he fell.

"Payday."

"Okay, it's in the locker, like last time. Now it's self service, though. Yank on the lock, it'll open. Put two hash marks beside the entry 'TX' in the book. TX is you.

"Don't fuck with the math. Don't fuck with anything. Two marks beside the others, and take two grams—that's it. Don't take more than two either, motherfucker.

"Push the lock back closed when you're done"

By that time, I would have dried my hands and have been heading down the ladder to the hangar bay and the mess decks below. I wasn't about to let hash peddling get between me and the mess decks.

I'd rather have lost money than missed my food.

Surprisingly, I think it worked fairly well. It's somewhat hard for me to really know, I guess. My margin on the sales was ridiculous. I had all the hash I could eat and/or smoke, and I put a few dollars in my pocket.

No. I didn't send those dollars back to Virginia, okay? I used them for, uh, "other" (limited) expenditures. Some vices are tough to abandon totally. Moderation: that's the key to prevent a total, cold turkey meltdown. Slow withdrawal, right?

I watched an A-7 go into the water. He was on the starboard side, maybe 3/4 of a mile out when we got word he was going to ditch. He didn't have a shitload of altitude when he punched, maybe 80 feet or so. A bit more than the height of the flight deck.

It was fucking cool.

The plane was cruising along and the canopy went, followed by dude's rocket chair. He came out clean with a full canopy following separation. The Corsair hit the water. The first touch, it belly skipped. When it went airborne once again, it got a fatal twist to the Y and X axes. On the second impact, it cartwheeled twice and was gone.

Fucking gone.

There was another that went into the drink, beyond the view of the ship. "Why" will never be known. It was said he just flew the damned thing straight in. He never radioed. He didn't attempt to eject. It would be like some guy driving his car into a pole on the side of the freeway for no apparent reason.

Only, there was nothing to clean up or haul off.

Gone. Fucking gone.

Any evidence to be gathered can be found on the bottom of the Mediterranean Sea.

I liked the little A-7s. They reminded me of MG sports cars. They were a one-man, subsonic aircraft; physically the smallest plane on the deck, yet one hell of a workhorse.

It wasn't their usefulness I liked them for, though. It was the way some of the jockeys would fly them over the ramp, still in the turn. It could freak a person out if they hadn't already witnessed it time and again.

The crazy bastards would still be lining up, port wing dipped, as they came over the round down. They'd line up on the center stripe, bring 'er back level and set it down. *Bang*, just like that! Damn, I always thought that was sweet! It was like having a playful dance partner up there. A-7s were just so… *precocious*.

You had to watch 'em though. They could get mean on ya.

The hook arm had a habit of smacking the fuselage when they engaged the Gear. To mitigate the damage, there was an impact pad fastened to the plane at that point. It was a chunk of yellow plastic about five inches in diameter and two thick. The center, at the fastening point, was thin. We called them doughnuts.

The hook arm would frequently dislodge the doughnuts. "Dislodge them," as in tossing a one-pound piece of plastic in your general direction at 150 mph. The bright yellow made them easy to see, so it wasn't a big deal. A bad bounce could catch you out, though.

I had one bounce about thirty feet in front of me. I could see it was going to pass just over my right shoulder. I reached for it. It would have been a sweet catch!

Zzzp, rrrrt, bzzzzt.

Those would be brain things firing off. One pound, 150 mph, thin leather glove with no fingers.

ABORT! ABORT!

I don't know that it would have removed my hand from the wrist, but I'm pretty damned sure it wouldn't have been pretty.

As I walked back to the Foul Line, I took a glance back at the Gear Puller. I knew he had witnessed the deal. I could read his lips as he pointed and mouthed, "You... *stoo*-pid... mother-*fucker*."

Another thing that bore watching was the turbine torque. Sometimes they'd come in and stay in the throttle a tad too long. That would twist them to port, sometimes with the starboard main mount leaving the deck. I've reached out for the wing and had it lift away from me, like playing Keep Away. If you were below that wing when it came back down...

There was the time I apparently wasn't paying close attention. When the underside of the wing forcefully whacked my helmet, it knocked me to my knees. It about knocked me out. That was embarrassing as all hell.

It's my job to pay attention.

I had one pilot come in and set his brakes while he was still leaning on the wire. I haven't a clue what was up with that cat. I don't know if he spilled his beer, dropped the roach, or what the fucking deal was.

There he was on the end of my wire, and he was looking around the deck of his cockpit. He wasn't looking at the Gear Puller. He was fishing around in there with his hook engaged at the end of the runout. I walked over and smacked the side of his airplane with my topside wrench. He looked up, startled, and I gave him the signal for "get your head out of your ass."

That would be one hand enclosing the other fisted hand. The fisted is withdrawn almost envisioning a sucking sound. I then gave him the hook-up signal.

Of course, being as he had screwed it all up, I had to give him hook-down, then a pull-back, and then another up. One plane got waved off. Sumbitch looked like he was in there trippin'.

Shit.

Still, Corsairs were my favorite plane. Tomcats were better for wing catching , but the A-7s were more fun to watch.

We had a wire break. It was at night. I, the Rabbi and some other cats are some lucky motherfuckers. We beat the long odds, baby.

I was checking Steve out on hooks, and we had transitioned into night ops. Steve had already expressed his dislike for running hooks after sunset. Some cats just don't care for dragons screaming at them out of the dark. We had just sat down together on the mess decks, when over the 1MC we heard, "Man all recovery stations. Man all recovery stations."

That meant some poor bastard was out there in a fucked-up airplane and needed to come home.

Now.

I snatched the fried chicken from my tray and jammed it into the right pocket of my jacket. I stuck a biscuit in the left. I eyed the mash potatoes and gravy, but thought better. You know the way of it by now. I wasn't going to miss a meal if I could help it.

We left our trays on the table and started yelling "MAKE A HOLE!" as we ran down the passageway and up the ladders. Our shipmates had heard the announcement and our greasy countenance identified us as "them." As we were suiting up in the shop, I handed the Rabbi the red flashlight we used at night.

"He's yours, man. It's a Tom with a hydraulic failure. He'll probably come in a little hot and his hook might not rise.

''I'm eating my chicken."

We ensured there was a full topside crew and headed up the Foul Line. We could already see his lights out there. The lights were a ways out, but he was coming. I found a nice shadow—an A-7 being between the tower, the meager lighting and me—and decided to start with a leg.

I took another look. He was a mile out. I could manage a couple of bites and swallows before he materialized.

He was in the short groove. I glanced at Steve. He was where he should've been. I put the remainder of the leg in my pocket. The bird trapped and began to run out. Steve had crossed the Foul Line and begun to approach him, red flashlight held aloft in the air.

Three-quarters of the way through its runout, the F-14's nose bobbed up.

It passed by Steve and shot off of the angle deck, headed for Davy Jones and his pals.

The pilot and RIO punched out.

Steve looked at me and yelled, "It wasn't my fault!"

You have no idea just how fucking funny that was. I yelled back, "The hook fell off!"

I'm not real sure who the straight man was in that exchange.

It was quiet, dead quiet as they brought up the lights. I looked aft. It was spaghetti back there.

We had broken a wire.

I can't begin to describe what that feels like. After I started running hooks, I used to have a recurring nightmare. It was more of a bother than a real problem. I'd have one version or another about once a month.

In the dream, something would have gone wrong and I dove to the deck. The threat would be over and I would start to regain my feet, only to discover my legs were gone. That would be the part where I'd wake up a bit out of breath. It wasn't a big deal, really.

We broke a wire.

I took my hands and gave myself a quick pat down. Head, arms, chest, torso… check. Legs?

Heh… legs!

I checked three more times. After that night, I never had the nightmare again.

The mess got cleaned up. It wasn't much really. No one—not one swinging dick—got hit by the wire. That is just about impossible.

If a flange in the hydraulic system of the engine let go, there was nothing to prevent the crosshead from smacking the fixed end of the machine.

That's game over, man.

See, something happened that theoretically shouldn't have. The CDP parted *at exactly the same time as a purchase cable below decks.* The energy in the cable died, not the men on deck.

Like I said, we beat the long odds.

As I had begun to say, the mess was cleaned up. The pilot and RIO got fished out of the drink, and we heard they hadn't received any major injuries.

It was time to go back to catching them, rather than putting them into the water, I guess. We were suiting up, getting ready to recover the regular Go, when a boot camp popped into the shop. He was kind of jacked up. He might have been in one of the dampers of the Two-blocked engine. The engine room was a mess. It wouldn't surprise me if there was wire on the deck in the sheave dampers, too.

So he asked, "Drift, man, how can you go back up there after what just happened? You and Steve should be dead!"

Fuckin' boots. Sheesh.

"See, you don't get it. I'm getting short. I'm down to like forty-five days. These cats have had all of this time to kill my ass, and tonight it was the Hail Mary.

"Yet here I stand. What do you think the odds of another break in the next forty-five days are?

"I'm leaving this grey bitch alive and whole. I got notice of that, just tonight.

"Here, pull my finger."

We were in port. I didn't have the duty, but I hadn't gone to the beach. I was lounging in the shop alone when Ruddy walked out of the office. He had a personnel file in his hand. It was mine, the name was in plain sight.

"You're getting short."

"Forty days, something like that," I responded a bit cautiously.

What the fuck now?

He pretended to be referencing what he had undoubtedly already read. I was afraid the Navy had caught the fact I had enlisted on a waiver (my previous admission to smoking weed), and then been busted. I thought maybe my separation was going to be fucked up (by the way, just the other day Fred told me he got popped *eleven times*).

"You never went TDY," he said, looking at me over his spectacles.

"Sure I did, man. I've been on the in-port fire party, side cleaners, duty driver..."

He gave me a wave of his hand, "No, dumbshit. I'm talking about when you reported to the ship. I'm talking about when you were a boot, before you went to a damper."

Well, he had me there.

I didn't know I had gotten away with anything at the time, so when I suspected I had, I just kept my mouth shut about it. Now here it was. It had apparently caught up with me.

There was no point in attempting a lie.

"No, I didn't do the mess decks or laundry when I reported to V-2. I came straight to the Gear."

"They want to send ya. They say everyone's got to do it."

He looked at me.

"I'm not going to let 'em. You don't send a short-timer to the scullery. I won't have it. Fuck 'em.

"You work for me; I decide where you go. You aren't going anywhere. Don't you worry about it."

I'm thinking old Ruddy was a fan of the Cap'n Drift show, as broadcast daily on the closed circuit TV.

At ten days out, I started running a short-timer's chain. A short-timer's chain is a set of light links worn from a key ring. Each link represents a day. I had a set of dikes in my shop locker that I used to clip one every morning. Sometimes to a fanfare.

It's an odd custom, I suppose, the short-timer's chain.

A chain was worn for no other purpose. One seen dangling from ones belt loop was a certain indication of their upcoming departure from the ranks of the United States Navy. Most guys started 'em at about twenty days. I started mine at ten. Given my normally modest demeanor, I certainly didn't want to appear ostentatious.

Three links left on the chain and I was awakened by Number Three taking a trap.

Fuck-oh-dear. I'm gonna be in a world of shit. What's happened?

Burnie would never allow me to stay longer in the rack than a half hour before the first launch. Launch, hell! Number three was retracting!

I'm in so much shit.

I tossed on my clothes and ran to the shop for my gear. Ruddy was watching traps on the TV.

"Damn, Ruddy… I'm sorry man. I don't know what the hell happened! I'm going, man. I'm going!"

I was tying off my wrench holster at the thigh when he said, "Take that shit off.

"Grab a cup of coffee. Have a seat."

Oh crap. This is going to be bad. I know it. Three days left and this is going to be fucking bad. Damn, I'm so fucking happy I'm out of here.

"I told 'em not to wake you. You are relieved of any and all duties until you land somewhere else.

"You're done. You can go on deck but you are hereby ordered not to run another hook. Not one.

"You've got three days left. It would be a shame to kill you now. Work with me on this. It's a quirk of mine."

Maybe he has his own nightmares.

"Who's running hooks?"

"Right now, the Rabbi," he said. "I think you taught him good, but he always has this touch of hesitation. Maybe he'll get more comfortable with time.

"C.O. is a lot slower, but you can tell that he has confidence. Cowboy is going to lose his fucking head if he doesn't slow down.

"I've watched 'em all at one time or another."

They're catching airplanes without me.

They didn't skip a beat. I was slightly devastated. I had to go back on deck. Cruising the machinery rooms was cool for a while, but then not, so I suited up and headed for Deck Edge.

I was just in the way. I wasn't interested in hanging out over on the platform. Besides, there were already enough people over there. There always were.

I stood with Burnie by the Number Three sheave for a while, but I felt like a spectator. I walked up the Foul Line and bullshitted with the fellas a bit, but the feeling was the same.

I'm a spectator.

So I went over to Cat Four and fucked up a launch.

I figured if I had've gone to the Cats rather than the Gear, I would've either wanted to work Hookup/Holdback or Safety. The Hookup and Holdback dude was the guy who slipped the launch bar (aircraft part) into the shuttle (the business end of the catapult), then hooked up the holdback.

The launch bar is most likely self-explanatory: put this plane part in that catapult part, then that catapult part will sling your ass off of the end of the angle deck.

You don't want that to happen until you want it to happen. That's what the holdback was for. On most (not all) aircraft, both devices were incorporated into the nosegear strut.

For most (not all) aircraft, the holdback consisted of a machined piece of metal. Imagine a small barbell but with sharp edges, not rounded. "Small," as in a man could hide it in his closed hand. That thin bit in the middle? That was the part that broke when the steam valve on the Cat was opened. That small bit of metal was all that held the aircraft in place as the Cat brought up tension and the plane's engines went to military power. Holdbacks were precisely machined to break under a calibrated load.

If the fellas on the Cat had a jockey who would routinely be a bitch getting set up, they would fuck with him with the holdback bar.

Because they could.

The way it worked was that Hookup & Holdback held the bar up to the jet jockey before going under the aircraft. The jockey was to both recognize its color (different colors, different aircraft) and general shape. After the pilot acknowledged that Cat dude had the correct device, Cat dude would flip it in the air, like a coin.

Once, catch. Twice... *oops*. To the deck it would fall. That bar was no longer precise. It had been compromised. Who knows when it might break? Cat dude would pick it up and duck under the plane with it, out of the pilot's line of sight. Cat dude would chuck it over the side, and take the good one out of his back pocket.

This is fun shit, ain't it? O' course the hookup would be made as usual. The catapult guys, all being in on the "bag," would watch the officer sweat in his cockpit. The man who believed his holdback had been dropped to the deck. The man who now was being asked to go to full power. The man who could abort the launch at any time. The man who had balls as big as church bells.

And they did. I never saw one give a thumbs-down. I did see sweat, but never a thumbs-down. Most got the hint, and weren't a further problem on the catapult taxi approaches.

I talked the guys on Cat Four into letting me hook one up. Playing Safety was out of the question. The Safety was the last cat guy to leave from under the plane's belly. His thumbs-up meant it was time to rock and roll. You didn't let inexperienced individuals perform that function.

I did talk 'em into letting me run an F-14 though!

The F-14's holdback was not like the others. It was some sort of reusable hydraulic device. Holding it upright, it came to about my belly button, maybe to the waist. It looked something like an oversized car shock absorber. They had a little window that showed red or green. Green was good for hookup, while red meant you had to beat it on the deck until you saw green. More than just a little green, apparently.

The Safety downed the Cat. The holdback device was showing half green, half red. I didn't know it had to be *all* green. I didn't even help them push the plane back off of the cat so the holdback could be cycled correctly.

Fuck that shit.

I was short. I went and got stoned. Real fucking stoned. I didn't have shit else to do—a "pushback" on a Cat was like a wave-off on the angle because the deck wasn't clear.

When ops for the day were done and the guys were in their racks, I went down to midrats, sipped on a glass of milk and poked at the eggs on my plate. They almost made me nauseous. I had a ticket in my pocket for a Greyhound that was leaving in the morning, and I couldn't eat.

Yeah, I know. It pissed me off, too.

I went back up to the shop. My sea bag was still sitting where I'd left it. I was wearing the working uniform I'd board the plane with, dungarees. I looked at the clock. Eight hours left. I sat in the dark for a short time, and then I said to myself, "Fuck this shit.

"One more bag. You need to get one more bag before you leave this grey bitch."

What to do? What to do?

I turned on the shop lights and looked around, hoping something would come to me. Time was short. My eyes settled on Cowboy's locker.

Cowboy had a locker below the work bench. Double-doored, it was a primo locker, really. You had to have had a bit of time under your belt to cop a locker like that. The doors were held shut by a lock passing through a tang protruding from both doors. To visualize the tang, take your hands and put them knuckle-to-knuckle with the fingernails pointed toward your face, fingers flat against one another. The lock would pass through the two securing them together. I laid a tiny weld bead, right where your little fingers would have met.

Taping his lock up out of my way, I knocked the paint off the joint with a file. I dragged the welding leads out of the barricade room, and laid one of the most beautiful overhead beads I've done in my entire life. When I cleaned up and dropped his lock back in place, there was no telling.

Come morning, I left on half the lights. I was sipping a cup of coffee, hiding in a dark corner, when Cowboy came tromping in wearing a tee shirt with a dungaree shirt over, a pair of drawers, a pair of socks and his boondockers. V-2 was to muster for inspection on the flight deck before Ops that morning—myself excluded, of course.

It was obvious that Cowboy kept his inspection pants in that shop locker.

Spinning the combo, he removed the lock and flipped it up on the counter (just like always), stood back and gave the left door a kick (just like always). Then it didn't open (*not* like always). He gave it another kick.

Nothing.

Now he was wondering what the hell was going on. He reached down to pull it open with his hands. That's when he felt it. He ran his finger down it. He couldn't believe it. He got down on the deck and looked at it.

With his attention on the locker, Cowboy still hadn't spied me in the dark. He had already been running late for inspection.

He stood up, picked up the lock, and threw it at the bulkhead with all his might.

"DRIFT, YOU *SON OF A BITCH!*"

I set my coffee cup down with enough force to catch his attention.

"You're hosed, man. I'm leaving off the bow in two hours. You'll never come up with a decent bag in that time. I win."

"The last bag is mine."

Cowboy was pissed. I mean really fucking pissed! I could tell by the way he was swinging the hammer against the chisel. I'm telling ya, it was one hell of a weld. I'm pretty sure he destroyed the tangs on his locker. I'm quite sure he was late for the muster.

I doubt very much that he told them I had welded his locker shut.

The End

We were to be the first or second launch of the morning. The birds were just beginning to fire off. They herded us out to make sure no one stepped in front of or behind something they shouldn't.

I stepped up the ramp into the C-2. I must have been toward the end of the line, because seating was getting scarce. I sat on the port side aisle, beside a Chief who had the window.

The seat faced aft, the front of the aircraft being to my back. I was looking out of the rear while strapping myself in and all of that good crap. Out there on the deck, the fellas were signaling goodbye.

Some were flipping me off. One was blowing me kisses and another grabbing his balls. The rest stood and smiled. The ramp started to close. As it was, I heard a man's voice. It was Lil' Ski, piping me off.

"*ding-ding-ding* … Cap'n Drift, departing."

I was already trying to deal with a bunch of water that was threatening to breach my left lower eye lid. Right about the time a single tear formed, the Chief beside me said, "Who the hell is *Captain Drift?*"

See, I had this fucking tear running down my damned face. And I was already having a hard time dealing with its treachery. I wanted to leave there. I'd counted a shitload more than ten days before I could leave there. I was only ever just visiting, see.

That ramp closes and that's it, I'm out of here, motherfuckers! I'm outta here…

I slowly turned to him. To the set of khakis in the window seat. I didn't wipe the tear. I didn't want to give either one the satisfaction, not the tear and not the Chief. My lip wasn't quivering. My eyes were clear and hard as diamonds.

There was no hesitation in my voice. It was firm and clear. "I'm Cap'n Fucking Drift, Chief.

"*I'm* Drift."

It was July 4th, 1979—Independence Day—when they shot me off the boat.

About Cap'n Drift

Drift has retired to the PNW where he lives in a small shack with his companion of 25 years. When he isn't pitching horseshoes, or sitting at the keyboard butchering the English language, he is active in prohibition reform. His views on the subject can be found at capndrift.wordpress.com

Look for his next work *From the Attic of a Madman?* in the near future. A collection of short stories written over several years, for the entertainment of friends and family.

About This Book

This book contains original material with all copyrights accruing to the author. Please do not distribute pirated copies.

This book was typeset in Adobe Garamond Pro, with headlines in Goudy Old Style. The cover and title were created by individually selecting letters from images of military stencils and are not a font.

Litsam titles are proofed through an innovative collaboration of readers and authors. The readers listed on the following page substantively improved this book by finding errors or offering editorial feedback. If you would like to know more about this new form of publishing, please visit www.litsam.com

Thanks and Appreciation

For editorial feedback and encouragement Jack Lewis, Lara Harriger, Rolf Vitous, and the entire WetLeather gang.

For quality assurance, Litsam thanks our Beta Readers.

In order of first report:

> Ted Timmons (21)
> Dean Woodward (3), editorial
> Shannon Kelley (27), technical (most impressive report)
> Rolf Vitous (6), editorial
> Lin Neighbors (5), design errors (most subtle errors)
> Kathy Gill (10)
> Lara Harriger (17)
> Glenn Stone (2), serial error & design error
> Roberta Mander Maghouin (6)

To WikiCommons and the U.S. Navy for the public-domain image of the USS America. R.I.P. USS America.

Author and rear cover images copyright Stone.

Shasta Willson for cover and interior design.

Made in the USA
Lexington, KY
03 September 2012